=:+:=:+:=:+:=:+:=:+:=:+:=:+:=:+

Your Habit Body

An Owner's Manual;

Gut-brain Axis 2.0

Bruce Dickson

=:+:=:+:=:+:=:+:=:+:=:+:=:+:=:+:=:+:=:+:=:

Revised second edition

Best Practices in Energy Medicine Series

HolisticBrainBalance.wordpress.com

3 of.

Your Habit Body An Owner's Manual,
Gut brain Axis 2.0

ISBN: 9798456138668

Revised second edition

The thing we are looking for,

is the thing we are looking with.

~ Ernest Holmes, Founder of Religious Science

The future is already here;

it's just not very well distributed yet

~ William Gibson, author, Neuromancer

https://HolisticBrainBalance.wordpress.com

Bruce also recommends http://MSIA.org

Your Habit Body - An Owner's Manual
Gut-brain Axis 2.0

Chapter 1

Can you pat your head and rub your tummy? ..17

Chapter 2

Our Habit Body is our very best friend...........31

Chapter 3
Sensory nature of our Habit Body 53

Chapter 4
We balance between habits (95%) and choice (5%)..55

Chapter 5

Traditional fairy tales about habits................68

Chapter 6

Four Anatomies of our Habit Body...................78

Chapter 7

Habits form around our five universal needs101

Chapter 8

Habits as "drama" 106

Chapter 9

Workable habits as "comfort zone"................113

Chapter 10

Our unexamined habits become our illnesses126

Chapter 11

Chapter 12

Chapter 13

Chapter 14
Why so difficult to change my habits?

Chapter 15
Why are addictions so addictive?

Chapter 16
Our habits around pain, PACME

Chapter 17
Holistic Practitioner topics

Chapter 18

Behaviorism - taking habits seriously 215

Chapter 19

Birth and death,...225

our two greatest learning experiences 225

Chapter 20

Frequently Asked Questions...........................231

Habits are conditioned behaviors given persistent substance in our psyche by repetition.

The waking adult psyche is composed of multiple energies. Each energy in our psyche--except free choice--can be conditioned into habitual behavior:

Lower Etheric energy (meridians, immune system)

Emotional energy

Mental energy

Mythological energy.

Q: How much of my waking psyche is composed of habits?

A: Bruce Lipton likes the 95% number. John-Roger likes the 90% number. Take your pick.

The topic of living as much as possible in the 5% to 10% of our waking psyche, which is free choice, is taken up in other titles in this series, notably in Balance on All Levels PACME+Soul. The present book attempts to expand known

concepts of habits into and towards a useful
Goethean Psychology.

Q: Why are my bad habits so persistent?

) 10% of us which
as effectively as we

/che. Western
ls only waking
rned a blind eye to
iple intelligences

)ke in the World
etlamp at night.

I recall a podcast of Dr. Christine Northrop where
she mentions a fruit flies experiment. In the
experiment young flies are put into a large, wide
mouth glass jar. The lid is no more than a clear
sheet of glass. Fruit flies have a short life cycle
measured in days.

After several days of flying around inside the jar,
the flies are mature. When the lid, the clear sheet
of glass is removed, do they fly out the top? Do

the fruit flies suddenly leave the jar? No. only one or two out of 50 flies will ever fly outside their old, established flying patterns.

They have been habituated to fly no higher than where they hit the glass--even when you take the glass away.

I also hear this is how fleas are trained for a "flea circus." They are habituated to jump no further than the boundaries they were habituated to. I am unsure where these experiments are online.

Please note this is NOT "instincts," this is clearly "habits" behavior conditioned to repeat, habits given substance by repetition.

Now apply this to human beings. This is how traditions get repeated, generation to generation. If you worship only the form of these traditions, you only worship the form, not yet the essence.

This is how traumas can become ingrained in us.

To clear these "bad habits," we have to--in consciousness--go down on one knee, lower our frequency until we find rapport with disturbed lower-frequency levels of intelligence. We learn what they are doing; we ask them how that's working for them. If they are willing to reform and upgrade, we suggest new behaviors and new role models likely to be more workable at their level.

This summarizes a very large fraction of all successful counseling and therapy across many modes.

Chapter 1

Can you pat your head and rub your tummy?

All men are similar. What distinguishes one from another is their habits

~ Confucius (heard from Derek Rydall)

Why do we have habits?

Human beings learn thru forming habits ~ Richard Bandler of NLP, heard in a podcast

Why are addictions—so addictive?

Richard Bandler, on the same podcast, says humans are very susceptible to addictions. To continue in paraphrase, forming habits is such a successful learning strategy, we learn all the time. Habits is how we learn physically, emotionally, mentally and unconsciously--on all levels. Habits is how new behaviors become part of our behavior repertoire.

If it's new behavior, maybe it's worth learning; I'll decide later. Some learning may not be useful later, but hard to determine this in the moment--so we learn whatever behaviors are repeated.

In this way we sponge up (learn) many behaviors "beneath our notice" without thought or examination: cursing, staying up late at night, eating junk food, eating candy, yelling at our kids, etc. As Habit Manager, Self is still responsible for any habits learned, no matter how learned.

95% of life is playing back habits on multiple levels, as useful to us. You walk, chew gum, hum a song all at the same time and think nothing of it. An old schoolyard challenge asks, "Can you pat your head and rub your tummy in a circle at the same time?" Most of our habit-combos are more subtle than this.

Most of what we do in life is multiple habits running simultaneously. Multi-tasking is indeed a sign of maturation. As we grow up and enter work life, the number and variety of habit-combos, behavior-combos, grows.

Study of our Habit Body answers the question: If our psyche is complex and wonderful, how come the one thing human beings do better than anything else--is make the same mistake over and over and over again?

Study of our Habit Body answers another tough question, "The main thing which was learned was—not much was learned" ~ Anonymous

See a way to make this material more accessible? Please contact the author.

"Habiting" per NLP and Wm. Glasser

As both NLP and William Glasser, author of Choice Theory suggest, the noun we call a "habit" is usefully viewed as a process: habiting: We go thru life "habiting" new behaviors into memory, into our Habit Memory, our Habit Body.

Learning any new task requires us to consciously and deliberately assemble a new set of specific behaviors. Learning to tie shoe laces in kindergarten is a classic new behavior worth children's time to learn. By the time we are five years old, we have thousands of routines and behaviors, including language, lodged in our sub- and unconscious as habits.

Learning how to create, save, abandon and retrieve a saved document in word processing is a classic new behavior worth an adult's time to learn.

Over time, with repetition, Conscious Self can pay less and less deliberate attention to sequencing the specific behaviors. In Three Selves terms, thru repetition and intention, basic self learns the sequence. In time, performing the sequence becomes more and more automatic. Habits is how we automate daily behavior.

The "invisible butler" did it

Our Habit Body is like an "invisible butler." We delegate performance of simple behaviors to him. Habits are our internal butler who carries out our wishes.

Notice your invisible butler can tie your shoe laces while you talk to a running mate. Your invisible butler remembers how you feel and think about certain people, places, things. An invisible butler remembers how you felt as a five year old.

What makes us truly human: courage, honesty, compassion, strength, resolve—are primarily invisible qualities. What else makes us human? Playing back complex sequences of habits. Guess what? Except in outer behavior, these are invisible too.

How can something so invisible also be so persistent and present? It's possible to ask a more therapeutic question: How come everyone grows up without knowledge of or methods to manage their own Habit Body? This book suggests how a future education can address many of the relevant issues.

Role of repetition in habits

A habit is conditioned behavior, conditioned to repeat. What we call "learning" is useful-workable conditioned behavior, repeatable on request.

Nothing can be sustained in our psyche unless and until it is repeated enuf times so our subconscious can attend to, grasp, and begin to imitate the behavior, copy it, thru practice, memorize it. All our good habits and all our bad habits are learned this way. No exceptions.

All human learning is based on repetition. We could say 90% or 95% of the contents of our waking human psyche is routine behavior conditioned to repeat; or more simply, habits.

Before learning, a void exists for those behaviors. Learning a new language for instance, if I intend to learn to speak French, I must practice and accumulate many habits of pronunciation, word use, definitions and so on--where previously no such habits existed in me.

Teaching an old dog new tricks, learning to ballroom dance after years of rock n'roll dancing-- or vice versa--is also learning yet perhaps less common.

Sometimes habits repeat over and over whether we like them or not. This verges on the topic of addictions. Smoking, uncontrollable anger. What emerged thru Internal Family Systems is how any behavior or habit which reduces internal hurt and shame is behavior we are likely to become addicted to.

To modify, re-direct or extinguish an unwanted habit, requires a healthy Self to manifest its intentions more strongly and more consistently than the "momentum" and "inertia" of an already-moving unwanted habit. Unburdening hurt and shame count for much, so does self-discipline.

This author's big battle with undesirable habits, was negative catastrophic fantasies. I had to stop and track down where each negative unconscious fantasy was coming from in my body; and, unburden this part of my psyche. This exercise was a big part of my own therapy. After 15 years, i've got these down close to zero. Daily mindfulness was required to identify, reduce and redirect this habit to a level where it no longer interrupted my inner contentment.

Unpacking "training periods"

To learn to ride a bicycle for the first time, to use roller skates for the first time, requires a period of time to train; everyone knows this.

WHY do we need a training period to acquire a new habit?

A computer does NOT need a training period to learn a new word processing program. You simply download or insert the program and open it up to use it.

Why are human beings not like this?

People are asking such questions because Western culture has been built on Descartes' idea, "I think, therefore I am." This approach is seriously outdated and no longer beneficial to progressive culture, since 1985; or perhaps, even 1970.

What if Descartes had said: 'I am 5% to 10% free choice; this is balanced in my psyche by 90% - 95% of learned subconscious and unconscious routines, held in memory. Therefore I don't have to re-learn how to talk again each morning.'

Do you think we might be further ahead now?

The above brings to mind, "I think, therefore I am." This was useful in its day. By 1945 it had outlived its usefulness. Women especially are impatient for men to catch up to where women are. I expect and look forward to women becoming much more articulate about their values and agendas in the next 100 years.

Perhaps Descartes might have said, 'It takes me time to learn how to ride a bicycle for the first time; because:

- First my conscious self has to get the concepts and perceive the structures are workable and reliable; then,

- I have to repeat the behaviors enuf times so my SUBconscious can learn them,

- Finally, I have to repeat the behaviors enuf times so my UNconscious can learn them.

In this way, I become UNconsciously competent and can ride a bike without thinking much and pay attention to the pretty girls walking by.'

Descartes was not able to say the above. In 100 years we will talk like the above as First Order Goethean Holistic Psychology spreads.

Habit is behavior running on a track

Any habit you can name is conditioned behavior—it's not completely free.

Our Habit Body can repeat a routine over and over, like an actor on Broadway playing the same role five nights a week and two matinees. If you change the track, the new behavior repeats along the new track, the new role.

Now-forgotten counseling therapy coined the idea "automatic thoughts" and "automatic feelings." The problem with this is it removes Conscious Self from responsibility for our actions and consequences. We wish not to excuse clients and therapists from our job as Waking Self, to acknowledge the consequences of our choices and actions; then, to manage excess and deficient liking and disliking habits ripe for re-direction today.

If we use mechanical ideas about "automatic behavior" to excuse ourselves from conscious personal responsibility-we weaken healthy Self-leadership.

Repeated behaviors are learned by the basic self. If practiced sufficiently, they are subsumed into our UNconscious habit repertoire.

In Waldorf child-development, children learn most of their habits thru imitative-thinking and taking-on-authority thinking. Our Habit Manager comes after puberty with independent and critical thinking.

Alchemy of habit formation

Habits are the result of converging two processes in our waking psyche:

1) Memories composed of multiple sensory percepts

2) Time, attention, repetition.

When a set of sensory percepts is repeated and attended to over and over, a curious thing happens. It's learned at deeper and deeper frequencies of our psyche.

The Conscious Self of a five-year-old sees an adult tying their shoe laces. If the five-year-old attends closely and accumulates accurate visual, auditory and kinesthetic cues, with practice, she can tie shoe laces "all by myself."

If she keeps tying shoe laces five or more days a week, for a few weeks, gradually the learning "sinks down" or "sinks in" to the sub-conscious.

Once a new behavior is successfully transferred to a child, such as how to put the cap back on the toothpaste, the routine sinks down and lives in the sub- and unconscious. Now we no longer have to think about it, or very little.

Adults call this, "I'm getting the hang of it. It's no longer so difficult for me. This is getting easier," and so on.

"As the twig is bent, so grows the tree"

Growth, good and bad, is easy to understand once we grasp the patterns afoot.

Elijah, my Native American Shaman friend, says the state of the fetus, in the womb, at six weeks, has already established many of the parameters of shape, flow and vitality which will be carried out until our dying day.

Doctor-hospital medicine talks about "birth outcomes" and how these have major influence over future health and development.

Waldorf education observes, in physical growth, after age seven, the human body primarily gains only height and weight. We primarily fill out whatever physical shapes we have by age seven.

Deficiencies are carried forward as we age; and eventually, can become more exaggerated. My grandmother had polio as a child in her leg. The partial shrinking of muscles in her one calf, due to polio, was particularly difficult to remedy as a child. Now in her 90s, the difficulties due to this condition increasingly bother her.

If left unchanged, disturbances on any level, PACME, can carry forward in our biography on each level as we age. Things which were a little out of balance mentally-emotionally as a child, if not remedied, may become exaggerated as we age.

That's why working on your bad habits, going after your issues early and pro-actively, instead of allowing them to age--is smart. Personal growth connects strongly with upgrading habits and behavior on any level, PACME. Any habit we perceive a deficiency in is fair game for improvement.

This book primarily concerns adult psyches. For children prior to puberty, we use the example of learning to tie shoelaces. It's a classic example of how habits form. After puberty, to some degree, adults learn in the opposite fashion. This tangential issue is taken up at length in the HealingToolbox booklet, *Human Learning Style Reverses at Puberty*.

Dictionaries define "habit" as a recurrent pattern of behavior, acquired through frequent repetition; a behavior pattern followed until it has become almost involuntary: the habit of looking both ways before crossing the street.

I like dictionaries in moderation. However, to compose a Three Selves view of habits, we have to go beyond most 20th century psychology.

e wrote and illustrated seminal book in my r" intuited correctly r generation to go urney far beyond the European Old World,

hed within a year of n Civil Rights in the

(1954), the decision widely regarded as having sparked the modern civil rights era. The Supreme Court ruled deliberate public school segregation illegal... ~ www.civilrights.org › Civil Rights History › Civil Rights 101

Chapter 2

Our Habit Body is our very best friend

Why do we have habits?

Learned behavior conditioned to repeat, is very useful.

When you get up to walk, how do you know whether to start with your right foot or your left foot first?

Getting up in the morning

Habits support us waking up in the morning already knowing how to put on our clothes and tie our shoes without re-learning these again each day. Our Habit Body stores every daily routine-- so we don't have to relearn each discrete behavior all over again each day.

"Getting up in the morning to go to work" is not one habit but many.

"Getting up in the morning to go to work" is a collection of habits on multiple levels.

From our neck up, we have the luxury of using language to throw all these habits into a single phrase, summarizing and generalizing 20-100 discrete practiced behaviors.

Do any two individuals get up to go to work, 100% identically? Probably not. We each have unique sets of habits around getting up in the morning: what nightclothes you take off first; which sock you put on first, getting dressed, eating, kiss the spouse, unlock the car, etc.

Learned behaviors conditioned to repeat serve us by allowing Conscious Self to perform many functions without a lot of intense, deliberate choice-making and decision-making. When the water boils, we turn off the stove. When the light turns green, we step on the gas. Much of each day is long strings of behaviors-habits where Conscious Self only makes minor adjustments to well-worn sequences of habits:

- getting dressed,

- eating breakfast,

- getting to work or school,

- eating lunch,

- coming home,

- nightly routines getting ready for bed.

Every day you perform these habits in similar sequences.

Every day you perform these habits and receive joy, goodness and learning, you build your Habit Body, reinforce those habits.

The habits you've used so far today, you probably prefer them in the sequence they occur. That's why you let them run on semi-automatic. When you come across an obstacle to your habit-string, you run out of toothpaste, you buy more. When you come across a better way to make your bed, you adjust your habit there and improve the excellence of the whole sequence.

For those looking for more precise metaphysics, our Habit Body is our etheric body. This is also the source of our capacity for multi-tasking--but I digress. Rudolf Steiner pointed out one of its natural, healthy intelligences is to want to do the same task better the next time. In this way, many of our habits evolve in a gentle upward spiral. Parenting can be like this. Romancing your partner can be like this. Improving your life can be like this.

Our Child Within, the basic self, can be conditioned to perform long strings of habit sequences. When added up, they comprise the majority of our waking time and behavior. This is most true for children.

In old-style factory-style public schools, kindergarten is often talked about among teachers as a year of learning procedures and routines which then carry forward into the grades. Waldorf whole-child schools delay this "hardening" of the Habit Body until Grade One. Prior to this, expanding play, rhythm and feeling Nature is emphasized.

Habits are neutral, neither good nor bad

Our Habit Body is neutral, neither good nor bad. If your habits are healthy and workable for you, you're happy with them. If your habits are unhealthy or many not working well for you, you're unhappy.

Our human experience is practice time making more healthy choices, which with practice, result in more good habits.

The above to some degree paraphrases William Glasser's *Choice Theory*. To paraphrase from Gerald Corey's *Theory and Practice of Counseling and Psychotherapy*, sixth ed. p. 230-233:

Choice Theory asserts the human being is not a blank slate, waiting for the external world to motivate us. Rather, Choice theory says all we ever do from birth to death is behave; and, all these choices are internally motivated, our best attempt to get our desired outcomes. "Every total behavior is always our best attempt to get what we want to satisfy our needs. [All] behavior is purposeful because it is [always] designed to close the gap between what we want and what we perceive we are getting.

Choice Theory allows only a very short list of mental illnesses, restricted to tangible, organic disturbances: Alzheimer's, epilepsy, head trauma and brain infections. Any other "mental illness" other than these are viewed by Choice theory as strings of choices made in concert with avoiding doing what we believe will not get our needs met. [Internal Family Systems adds: behaviors which, no matter how bizarre-seeming to others, temporarily reduce hurt and shame in the doer.]

Alternatively, mental-emotional disturbance not due to organic dysfunction, can be strings of choices, made in concert with having no strategy (no ideas) how to move forward and towards getting our immediate needs met.

Tangentially, this is where Rudolf Dreikur's four mistaken goals of (discouraged) children has its place. But I digress.

Glasser speaks of people "depressing" and "angering" themselves rather than "being depressed" or "being angry."

When people allow, promote or choose unhappy behaviors, this is simply the best coping option they had on hand, at the time.

Depressing (undercharged habits, undercharged liver) is the most common way people have found to ask for assistance without begging.

Angering (overcharged habits, overcharged liver) is another popular way people ask for assistance without begging.

Angering is also a way to push away a frustrating relationship and establish a new interpersonal boundary where none existed before. Angering may be a primitive response; it may not be the most effective response. In the moment, it may be the only response a person has to a frustrating situation.

We're all here learning to become better Habit Managers

In terms of personal-spiritual growth, the good news is we can drive a car and talk hands-free on the phone at the same time; usually, without wrecking the car.

The good news is complex behaviors and strings of simple behaviors can be transferred downward, out and away from Conscious Waking Self, towards SUB- and UNconsciousness which we term the Habit Body.

The bad news? Once behaviors are transferred downward and further away from Conscious Self, they are more difficult to alter, change and upgrade.

In a nutshell, this is why habits are challenging to change, they no longer exist in the wheelhouse of the Conscious Self. They now exist and have their life outside the wheelhouse of the Conscious Self.

To access them, they are no longer "at hand." You alter them, you find them, go to where they live, negotiate with them again.

Everyone has a Habit Body; so, we may as well talk about it.

How we perceive a habit

Here's a common way we encounter our Habit Body. I was walking to my locked car (any locked door). I reached into my pocket for my keys. I vaguely looked at them. When I arrived at the door, I was holding one single key at the ready. However, I was not holding the correct key for this door.

Without looking, without the monitoring-editing function of Conscious Waking Self, my Habit Body got all the way to readying a key for the door. I honor it could do all this on its own. It still needed my collaboration to discern the one correct key for this door. That's not a problem; that's teamwork.

Habit Body and conscious-waking mind often meet in the gap between habits which almost work "automatically" but which need a bit more clarity, objectivity and preciseness to work all the way.

Your Habit Body is smart enuf, on its own, to access "a key" to address a locked door. However if a key ring has many keys on it, it may not be smart enuf to access the correct key on its own.

You, waking-conscious self, has the high-frequency intelligence required to discern which key fits exactly which door.

Such inner cooperation is healthy and desirable. In this way our two lower selves work as a team.

All our habits are like speech accents

Another way people focus on their Habit Body is speech accents, your accent and other people's accents.

Dictionary.com says an accent is "the unique speech patterns, inflections, choice of words, etc., identifying a particular individual or national speech pattern."

I believe, this conventional definition both over-shoots and under-shoots the learned behaviors playing back in accents.

Clearer language might be, what we perceive when listening to a noticeable Scottish or East Indian accent to their English, is a person speaking English with traces of old speech habits are demonstrating speech habits exist on a range of levels between conscious Self and our Habit Body. The levels closest to Conscious Self are easier to change; they change first. The deepest levels of Speaking in a second language can remain imperfect for decades. Only movie actors, usually with a speech coach, have the opportunity and resources to unlearn their deepest old habits and re-learn new deep speech habits. Speech coaches get your full and complete attention to tongue, teeth and breath use and placement.

Unwanted speech accents are difficult for speakers to change because each speaker does not hear their own speech as different or foreign in any way.

The challenge of changing your speech accent points up ALL our habits are like this, learned sub- and unconscious behavior which "come to light" when it conflicts with the habits of other people.

How are habits stored in my body?

The Habit Body model is the sum and the repository of all habits, in one individual, PACME.

In this model, habits are NOT stored in our meat-bone body. They are stored in our pre-physical body, the "other half" of our physical body, our invisible etheric body.

A healthy etheric body remains in close connection and relationship with our physical body. Functions of our "etheric body" overlap up to 90% with our "immune system." 100% of our Habit Body is in theta and delta brainwave frequencies.

Where is reactivity stored in my body?

Reactivity primarily originates in the sub-conscious and unconscious levels of the solar plexus. The little circle below marks your belly button.

Identifying and locating reactivity is taken up much more thoroly in Inner Family + Inner Court; The Four Archetypes of Our Gut and Head. The Babinetics model locates where reactivity is relative to the body.

Reactivity is primarily in the sub-conscious and unconscious levels of the solar plexus (Bertrand Babinet):

Simplified geography of reactivity

SUBCONSCIOUS

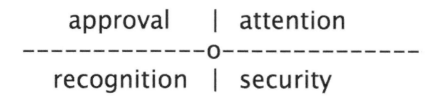

Liking and disliking occur equally in the subconscious above the belly button and in the unconscious below the belly button

This diagram is useful for locating where a disturbance is relative to the front of the human body. For a fuller discussion of this and all related matters, see The Inner Court, Close-up of the Basic Self. This is 400 to 600 level material. Identifying, locating and characterizing reactivity is taken up much more thoroly here.

Q: Can you put this in behavioral terms?

Liking and sympathy for something, like food, is good—too much liking and sympathy can become a problem.

We respond with liking and sympathy for those things we wish more of inside our comfort zone.

Disliking and antipathy can be good, such as saying "no" to high commercial bank charges by switching all your money and accounts to a credit union. Too much disliking and antipathy against the IRS or the government can get you put in jail.

We establish disliking and antipathy against because we wish to protect our Self. We wish for fewer and less unwanted things inside our comfort zone.

Reactivity can be looked at as excess sympathies and antipathies, excess liking and disliking.

You won't be surprised to hear doctor-hospital medicine does not support this idea. You won't be surprised to hear doctor-hospital medicine has its own meat-bone ideas about how habits and memory are stored in anatomical structures.

The latest physical approximation of an etheric reality is the "basal ganglia." I believe the original 2011 Nature article is "The role of the basal ganglia in habit formation" by Henry H. Yin and Barbara J. Knowlton

http://www.im-clever.eu/documents/courses/computational-embodied-neuroscience-1/CEN/files/YinKnowlton2006RoleOfBasalGangliaInHabitFormation.pdf

Check it out and tell me if the Habit Body model is more or less workable for you.

An easier model of our unconscious

I believe for many,"Habit Body" is an easier, clearer concept than "basal ganglia" or "unconscious."

Dictionary.com says the term "unconscious" comes from 1705-1715, a time when our unconscious was literally inaccessible by any therapeutic method whatsoever. Since muscle testing met NLP around 1990, our unconscious has become much more accessible, for those who wish access.

"Unconscious" connotes "unknowable." Since 1990 or earlier, our unconscious is knowable, is accessible, to those who wish to access it; and, who keep up to speed with developing therapeutic methods in this field. So we need a more accessible word and model for our unconscious.

A "Habit Body" connotes " I can change this, if I want to." This is true now, for those looking for it.

Reactivity is excessive and for ourselves dysfunctional responsiveness. You get a letter in the mail from the IRS and you freeze up. Relax, it's only a generic description of your benefits.

Why did I freeze up? Where did my reactivity come from?" Well, let's think it thru. Does it come from the dim above or the dim below? The dim below. Habits and reactivity come from the basic self. The basic self is our "Habit Body."

Habit Body as Reactivity—another best friend

We've said habits are behavior set on automatic, learned behaviors conditioned to repeat.

Let's expand "habits" to include "reactivity." If we do, we have found another good friend of Conscious Waking Self. Or maybe you prefer "reactivity" as another two-edged sword capable of cutting to the good or to the bad?

A sad conventional wisdom is often heard, "If people knew better, they would DO better." More precisely we can now say, 'If a person's Habit Body knew how to do better, the person would do better.'

What's sad to me is not that "people do not do better;" rather, how little intention, time and effort individuals put into exploring their own Habit Body; and then, upgrading outworn and obsolete memories, habits, behaviors and expressions they find there.

I'm going to say something next that may only become clear at the end of this book. It needs to be said here because it is the key people are looking for and its natural place comes at the beginning—once you have eyes to see it.

Maturing up includes making more and better distinctions between who "I" am; on one hand and, my expression in this world thru my Habit Body, on the other hand.

Perhaps this is clearer: Maturing-up includes making more and better distinctions between myself as a capital "S" self, me as soul, on one hand and, who "I" am here in this 3D world, the small "s" self, my expressions, habits and behaviors, on the other hand.

The following is from the booklet, *Willingness to Heal Is the Pre-requisite for All Healing*:

Reactivity is a two-edged sword. If we did not react, if you were crossing a street on foot and saw a car bearing down on you, without reactions, you would have to think, "Now what, if anything, does this have to do with me?"

If our spouse smiles and touches our arm in a soft and gentle caress, without reactions we would only be able to think, "Now why is he doing this?" With reactions we move first, think later. Reactivity has its uses. If we are smart, we give our reactions their due and use them to our advantage.

The game is not to eliminate reactivity: rather, to moderate EXCESSIVE reactivity, unnecessary over- and under-reacting to our self other people, the world.

Excess reactivity as excess-liking & excess-Disliking

Excess reactivity can be viewed as excess sympathies and antipathies, excess likes and dislikes.

Rudolf Steiner suggests the work of growth is largely, "reducing our excess sympathies and antipathies." That's a fair definition of personal growth. It's in concert with removing the big rocks of reactivity first if you wish to clear a path of your own growth.

We can react with either sympathy or disgust. We may react sympathetically as in, I like it." Or we may react with antipathy, as in, "I don't like it."

Ambivalence and confused reactions arise when we have both sympathy and antipathy towards the same thing, like towards Mom, for instance.

With excess sympathy, we favor things even when they are bad for us. The inner child says,

"Chocolate cake would taste so good!"

The conscious yak-yak mind says, "I'm on a diet."

The body, the gut brain says, "But the cake would taste so good!" We all have parts who lead us to choose behaviors unauthorized or distasteful to our conscious self.

With excess disliking, we react to things unfavorably, even when the thing is healthy. The two year old says, "I hate spinach." The twenty year old says, "I hate putting money in my savings account." The sixty year old says, "I hate exercising."

Rudolf Steiner's offhand definition of growth as "Overcoming our excess sympathies and antipathies," points to the biggest category of disturbances we have to deal with while on Earth.

Until we can get beyond, "I knew it was wrong and I did it anyway," more subtle wisdom remains elusive. The biggest Job in self discipline is disciplining our reactivity.

If growth is your game, your best friend is reactivity.

Why? Because our over-reactions point very directly to the next habits Life is asking us to address, retrain and upgrade.

Find and release your excess reactivity and you are that much closer to peaceful, productive times.

Being of two minds is a top-bottom split

When someone is of two minds, this is never a vertical split but always a horizontal split: The cerebral nervous system has one point of view, one goal. When enteric nervous system is not aligned, it has diverging feelings over a different need, another priority.

The conscious yak-yak mind says, "I'm on a diet."

My body, my gut, my gut brain says, "But the

cake would taste so good!" We all have parts who lead us to choose behaviors distasteful to our conscious self.

'Dysfunctional responsiveness' is another way to language excessive reactivity. You get a letter in the mail from the IRS and you freeze up. Relax, it's only a generic description of your benefits. Why did I freeze up? Where did my reactivity come from?"

If growth is your game, modulating and re-calibrating your reactivity, as life gives you opportunity, keeps reactivity a good friend and not an enemy.

Our over-reactions today point directly to the next habits Life is asking us to address, retrain and upgrade.

Find and adjust your excess reactivity and you are closer to peaceful, productive times.

You've heard, "If you can feel it , you can heal it."

Habit Body as "response-ability"

Our ability to respond to our environment and to others, responses at the ready, is our Habit Body.

Before I went into private practice seeing clients, I was co-teaching a class of severely autistic teenagers. Autistic kids love habits and predictable routines. I had solved the problems of my job to a very high degree. I had a large and complete set of habits to make the class run well for myself, students and aides. One day I realized things ran so smoothly, I could simply send my habits to work. My "I" did not have to go in. As long as I continued running the healthy habits, things would go well. My success at my job was largely a matter of running a set of healthy habits.

What happened? The administration moved me to a classroom of younger children to solve a problem they were having. I had to consciously rethink all my habits to create healthy solutions for this new set of circumstances. And so it goes.

This verges on the topic of "phoning in a performance," where only habitual behaviors are evident to an observer without the creativity and spark of Imagination, Inspiration, Intuition.

Two biggest habits of all: safety and trust

Some say our Habit Body is conditioned about 95% by age three. I agree with the observation.

I imagine we learn a great deal about how safe we can feel and how much we can trust, in our third trimester in-utero thru age three.

Up to three years old and often longer, many basic habits are established around learning what is safe and who we can trust. If this still sounds odd, imagine how much infants and the very young child are attuned to safety and trust.

Feeling safe or not-safe in our immediate environment,

trusting or not-trusting those around us.

This is most of what we do from infancy to age three. If we do experience a modicum of safety and trust, the main habit change is expanding language-vocabulary.

We call these "survival skills."

More nuanced, sophisticated language about unresolved disturbance often overwhelms and obscures a more basic issue: Do I feel safe with X? Is X trustworthy for me now, in this situation?

Habits of safety and trust formed in utero

Gabor Mate tells a story on a 2013 audio from a live talk of babies in utero. He says the fetus is constantly asking the mother, "How safe is the world I will be born into?" The mother answers the fetus chemically by her cortisol levels, her stress hormone levels.

When the fetus senses stress hormones, it builds up its own rear brain, the reptile brain, its natural fight or flight mechanisms.

If the mother's stress hormones are low, the fetus perceives the world as safe and builds up the forebrain, the neocortex, our naturally more artistic and creative and executive portions of its brain.

Much more can be said about our habits around "safety" and "trust." These are often unexamined; and therefore, become stumbling blocks.

Third biggest habit: social permission

Between three and seven years old, we learn a ton about which behaviors are and which behaviors are not permissible around our family, at school, at church, and so on. This topic verges on how every local culture is simply another basket of discrete behaviors on which wide consensus exists locally.

Chapter 3

Sensory nature of our Habit Body

Booklets 24 and 25 in Best Practices in Energy Medicine together cover what we know about the senses in the field of Energy Medicine.

#24) *From 5 to 12 Senses, How We Use Multiple Senses to Triangulate, Multiple Intelligences 2.0 -* 10,800 words

#25) *VAKOG to KAVOG, NLP Senses Updated in Light of the Inner Child*

Senses in our Habit Body tend to be arranged top to bottom not VAKOG but KAVOG

Briefly, our meat-bone body has sensory organs. If they are healthy, our etheric body receives sensory percepts thru each and all of these sensory channels.

In waking adults, these sense percepts are available for rational feeling and thinking. I like it; I don't like it, etc.

The same sense percepts are also available to our Habit Body. Then what happens? Often reactivity results: I hate you! Oh, no, this depresses me even more. Pardner, them's fighting words to me and my posse! Chocolate cake?! My favorite!

In adults, Conscious Waking Self has the job of moderating-managing our responses to sensory percepts we receive.

Not to go too far afield, memories are a category of habit which our Habit Body stores. To paraphrase NLP, we store memories using "video compression software." NLP calls this software "deletion, distortion, omission." To this list we can add "exaggeration." Tall Tales are found in comedy routines, funny stories and so on.

Chapter 4

We balance between habits (95%) and choice (5%)

Bruce Lipton and others say only 5% of our psyche is capable of exercising conscious waking choice and deliberate decision-making. In Three Selves terms, that's us, from the neck-up, Conscious Waking Self.

You and I, Conscious Selves, we're the Habit Sequencers, the Behavior Schedulers, the Habit Managers and Superintendent of Behaviors.

Bruce Lipton puts a number on how much of our psyche is composed of habits: 95%. He estimates the remaining 95% of our psyche is composed of habits.

Bruce Lipton does yet use the term, Habit Body. He approaches the idea and the phrase very closely in this 30 minute podcast talk:

http://www.podcastchart.com/podcasts/art-of-joyful-living/episodes/dr-bruce-lipton-spontaneous-evolution/pop

Two indivisible units in our psyche

If we use the term "Habit Body," then we can posit a clear, simple polarity of two indivisible units in our psyche. On one side, Free Choice; on the opposite side, our Habit Body, the sum of all our learned behaviors conditioned to repeat.

Definitions

A Habit in psychology is (1) any regularly repeated behavior, requiring little or no conscious choice to perform or express, (2) any repeatable behavior, whether currently expressed or not, which has been learned and stored in memory.

In the human experience, "habits" are often opposed to, or complemented by, "free choice."

A Choice - Conventional definitions of "choice" as "the act of choosing" are accepted here.

When we're not making decisions-picking-choosing, our behavior is mostly playing back from our Habit Body, our rich library of learned-conditioned behaviors. The combination of choice and playing back learned behaviors, on many levels, is how we make our way thru our day, each day.

Seesaw of habits~choice

r like two
teeter-totter.

king,
ecisions.

Perhaps surprisingly, the 5% of our psyche
capable of deliberate conscious choice, can
balance the other 95% of learning behavior
conditioned to repeat.

As a see-saw goes up and down,

back and forth,

two opposing forces,

the human experience

is balanced between, on one side

habits, behavior conditioned to repeat,

to get us thru our day; and,

on the other side,

making conscious, deliberate choices

about what we want more of and what we want less of, how we will achieve our goals and get our needs met.

How can 5% of my psyche balance 95%?

As seen by the Angels, your 5% carries as much "weight" as the other 95% of your psyche.

Exercise your 5%, and it builds up and "out-weighs" the 95%.

How is this possible? You're not helpless. You are Choice. The human experience is designed for soul to exercise free choice (not 'free will').

Why? Soul is choice. You can change any unwanted or corrupted habit simply choosing anew. Sometimes choosing a new habit consciously, for 32 days in an unbroken row, is needed to break an old habit and establish a new habit.

Our 5% ability to choose anew and make decisions, is what stands-in for our eternal-immortal soul, here in the human experience.

Soul is choice.   "Don't leave home' without it (choice)."

Q: If my Habit Body is doing 95% of my behaviors, what's left for me to do?

A: You and I, Conscious Selves, we're the Habit Sequencers, the Habit Editors, the Behavior Schedulers and Superintendent of Memories. In life we initiate new learning, towards creating new habits, upgraded habits. We maintain workable habits. We decide when NOT to express a habitual behavior no longer workable for us.

That's our genius as Conscious Waking Self, to make healthy choices and decisions every day. Any of this starting to sound familiar?

As Plato or Socrates said, "to make the right decision, at the right time, with the right person, for the right reasons."

You and I, Conscious Selves, we're the Habit Sequencers, the Behavior Schedulers, the Habit Managers and

Choice as independent-critical thinking

Only 5% of Choice is powerful enuf and free enuf to balance 95% of habits conditioned to repeat.

This is why independent thinking, learning how to think for yourself, critical thinking, is so crucial after puberty. This is why Waldorf educators are so keen to support children evolving into thinking for themselves, independent thought. In thinking for yourself, in Choice, we are Kings and Queens.

I don't feel like I even have 5% choice

Many women may feel this way in dysfunctional Patriarchy cultures, including the USA in early 2017.

In this case, I have good news for you. Did you know modern psychology, thru MBTI, since about 1990 considers both "feeling" and "thinking" as "rational functions." See Lenore Thompson's *Personality Type, an Owner's Manual* (1998).

So when reading if an author writes "thinks" or "thinking" if Feeling is your preferred rational mode, you can substitute "feels" and "Feeling" and you may find more sense in this.

Not in Lenore's book, is a new idea in MBTI. If we add a dimension of "maturity" to the 16 types, rational Feeling tends to be more mature than rational Thinking. Why? Because rational Feeling is more likely to incorporate and integrate compassion and empathy than Rational Thinking.

Generally adults make choices and decisions from the neck up. If you dislike this characterization, the more accurate and precise anatomy is: we are rational primarily from above our diaphragm muscle, heart, pericardium, lungs, and up.

If I thought more average readers even knew where their diaphragm muscle is, I would be tempted to use a more precise anatomic location.

In the 1890s Rudolf Steiner likened, what we in modern terms would call, Conscious Waking Self, to a gentleman riding in a horse-drawn carriage. The horse and the wheels of the carriage go up and down over the bumps and navigate unpaved roads and bumpy cobblestone roads; while, the gentleman riding in the carriage—especially if the carriage has good spring suspension—experiences many fewer and much milder bumps and interruptions to his quit process of inner thought and feeling. I think the major exposition of this is in RS's 1919 Study of Man.

When the 95% overwhelms the 5%

The seesaw image suggests "balance." When our 5% of healthy Self is out of balance, it can easily feel overwhelmed and swamped by what habits the Habit Body plays back over and over and over. When our healthy Self 5% gives up, it allows old habits to continue playing back thru our day.

Our Habit Body is vast—but our immortal-eternal soul aspect is even more vast—if you as Choice claim and sit on the throne of your own waking experience.

If you ever feel overwhelmed with too many decisions, if you ever feel tired as a decision maker, this is not an illusion. Conscious waking Self has need for rest, nourishment, support and down-time. These are real needs.

5% as "conscience"

Our healthy Self 5% in its positive and healthy habits and connections with Higher Guidance is what develops into "conscience."

In Three Selves terms, our "conscience" is a 'moral flywheel' of habits whose comfort zone is truly human values.

Angel~devil on your shoulders

ividual wrestles
ople, one an
ter's

on the right
e left shoulder.
ch other or talk
sation.

pposite
to truly
human values; or, acting selfishly.

You in the middle, Conscious Waking Self, are the observer. You get to decide which one to listen to.

In the Shadow chapter, we quote from the TV Tropes website. It offers a list of narrative devices which if not used skillfully, towards meaning, feeling and insight, come off as cliches.

Is "Choice vs. Habit Body" the same as "gut brain axis"?

Yes, analogous. "Choice vs. Habit Body" is the same as "gut-brain axis." Which language do you prefer? Which seems more complete and workable for your needs?

Q: Isn't, "The human being is just a bunch of habits" the worst 1930s deterministic behaviorism?

A: If you stop there, define the waking human experience as habits and nothing more, as only the 95%, then yes, you align with BF Skinner and deterministic Behaviorists, of the 1930s.

This is again why the 5% is crucial. If no 5%, if no good Angel on your right shoulder, you are not much better than animals who choose selfishly.

Only soul—however individually conceived—can balance all the pre-determined conditioning family, world and culture give us. Soul permits us "free choice" within local parameters.

Our life runs mostly on automatic unless and until each of us consciously chooses to isolate a bothersome habit; then, take time to upgrade and redirect it. You can upgrade habits on any level of concern to you.

Is our reptile brain our Habit Body?

No but it is part of our Habit Body.

In his original three selves seminar, circa 1971 in San Francisco, for MSIA.org, John-Roger specifies "spinal reflex thinking" as part of the basic self. Spinal reflex thinking may or may not be identical with our "reptile brain." The two certainly overlap. Our reptile brain is intelligence limited to survival issues: warmth, food, comfort and reproduction. This deeper level of habits, closer to needs, will run us if we let it. Like any other level of habits, it will play back learned habits unless-until redirected.

Multiple Intelligences 2.0 suggests we think our our psyche as many layers of intelligence, stacked up. This is how to avoid the George W. Bush error, thinking you are ONLY the "Decider and the Completer" and nothing else. Like every smart phone and every piece of complex electronics, you have multiple centers of intelligence and processing.

Habit Body as instincts?

Instincts are real for all animals and insects, etc because this is the highest frequency of intelligence they possess.

Guess what? Instincts are "less real" for adult humans because we have many layers of intelligence of much higher order than instincts.

Animals are designed to function "on automatic." Human beings are designed to function thru choice.

Animals' ability to learn is curtailed by how quickly instincts dominate their awareness. Humans ability to learn and adapt is prolonged by a very long infancy, childhood and adolescence, compared to animals.

Consider a balance scale: The more weight we give instincts in people, the more choice is eroded.

Instincts are "hard wiring" in the psyche whereas habits are closer to "programs." Programs and habits can be changed by re-choosing, time and attention.

Other views of 95% vs. 5%

John-Roger suggests 90% of our psyche is habits. If you like 10% of us is Waking Conscious Self— no problem: A Habit Body is an easy way to think about the 90% of us conditioned by repetition.

The Conscious Self's role in habit formation is to allow, promote and create new and healthier habits. Conscious Self is the educator of the basic self.

Chapter 5

Traditional fairy tales about habits

I made my living for ten years telling stories in public schools as a "super substitute" teacher who brought their own material with them.

I'm aware of three famous fairy tales about our Habit Body. All use a similar motif. All dramatize how wonderfully abundant--or abundantly pernicious—habits can be, when behavior repeats over and over.

Grimm's "Sweet Porridge" highlights a magic cooking pot. It produces cooked porridge (oatmeal) whenever a magic formula is spoken. Sweet porridge is enjoyed until a user forgets the magic formula for making it stop. The pot continues producing porridge until a tsunami of porridge is unleashed on the countryside. Is this the pot's fault? It was simply following instructions: make porridge.

The moral of this tale? Habits are behavior conditioned to repeat; be careful which habits you set in motion. How to end a habit is equally meaningful with setting one in motion.

Grimm's' "Sweet Porridge" bears a close resemblance to "sorcerer's apprentice" tales (motif type 325 in fairy tale scholarship): a naive helper charms a broom into carrying water correctly--but then--cannot make it stop because he does not know the correct charm. Goethe published a ballad of this 325 type in 1798.

From a Three Selves point of view, both "Sweet Porridge" and "Sorcerer's Apprentice" fairy tales point to our less conscious habits, those difficult to access—but if and when you do—watch out! The results can be magical—either positively or negatively!

The Sorcerer's Apprentice motif points to the magical nature of our Habit Body. It warns us not to trifle with our magical nature; unless, we are as good at stopping a spell as we are at starting one.

Maturity and wisdom is needed to handle the Habit Body, visible in the person of the older sorcerer, in the Disney cartoon version. The story highlights you have to know how to speak with the Habit Body, in the special way it can hear and respond to. In our deep unconscious:

It does not work the way we THINK it works;

it does not work the way we WANT it to work;

it does not work the way we WISH it to work.

It pays no attention to what our rational mind--thinking or feeling--from the neck up.

It works the way it works in a frequency of intelligence quite distant from the comfort zones of Waking Self.

How our deeply unconscious Habit Body works, its terms, its mechanism, can be known. Learning these terms is rare because few wish to journey there. Why? Humility, gentleness, safety, trustworthiness are the pre-requisites.

The hidden nature of the Habit Body changed rapidly once Touch for Health popularized muscle testing in the 1970s. In parallel, NLP began getting serious about documenting Unconscious Patterns, how to access them, how to alter them therapeutically.

Still the cautionary tale of the Sorcerer's

Apprentice still holds: 'With great power goes

great responsibility' ~ Spiderman.

Maglc Salt Grinder "put right"

The fairy tale connecting these motifs and the Habit Body for me was "Why the Sea is Salty" (motif type 565). An okay print version of the tale is here: http://park.org/Korea/Pavilions/PublicPavilions/KoreaImage/hangul/litera/mill/index.htm

How our unconscious functions, as viewed from the unsophisticated conscious self, is colorfully pictured in fairy tales of the salt-grinder at the bottom of the sea, "Why the Sea Is Salty."

Did you know there was a time before all the oceans of the world were salty? Here the magic implement is a salt mill which, once started, continues turning out salt, until a certain command it can understand is given.

Before the salt grinder turned the sea salty, we infer from the fairy tale, the sea was useful, drinkable, FRESH WATER.

Turning it to SALTwater is an error, an accident, a tragedy: a large body of fresh drinkable water has been polluted with salt and made undrinkable.

Consider a magic grinder. It does not start out to grind salt endlessly and wreck a freshwater ocean. The fairy tale tells us, "It looked like any other stone hand mill but it had special powers. All one had to do was say what one wanted and turn it. Out would come what had been requested.

If gold was requested, gold would come out. If rice was requested, rice would come out. Whatever was requested, the small hand mill would produce it."

This is the cornucopia, Horn of Plenty motif, images for the power of our unconscious mind set free from all narrow boxes; and then, linked with archetypal Abundance.

The fairy tale entices us to conjure with harnessing the power of our unconscious, releasing learned restrictions put on us, so we again have a magical servant, who can manifest whatever is needful.

The magic grinder is not owned by a peasant or wood cutter but by a king, someone wise enuf to understand and respect the potential for good and harm inherent in a magic salt grinder, our habit body.

The King only asks the grinder to make what is needful, for the highest good, only when it is needed, for the highest good of the entire kingdom.

The precise form of the effective command to stop is of interest in this tale: "Mill, mill, stand still, for I want nothing more!"

In Three Selves terms, the conscious self has to step in and command a cessation of activity, must consciously redirect activity on the level of the mill clearly, directly, explicitly.

In the tale, a thief steals it; sells it to a new owner, a boat captain, who cares little about the magic phrase. The captain is unable to stop the mill as his boat fills up with ground salt and sinks the boat. The captain throws the mill into the ocean, where it continues to grind out salt infinitely forever—and this is why the sea is salty.

The thief and the sea captain both lack kingly discernment. They know only greed. The grinder goes rogue due to untamed greedy-thinking.

The endless, mindless salt grinding, salt-making, points to the repetitive cycling nature of habits, once set in motion. They do not stop—until the rational mind engages and understands the language of the habit at its depth.

From freshwater to tears

The tale highlights the change in quality of a large body of water, from fresh water to salty, undrinkable water. Sea imagery in fairy tales points to the emotions and/or the huge uncharted realm of our unconscious.

That one habit, done for thousands of years, altered the taste and drinkability of all water everywhere equally, tells us about the power each habit has to alter the inherent happiness of our etheric body into sorrow.

How do we get down to the grinder and re-program it to grind fresh, sweet drinking water, instead of salt? How do we reverse the process and turn a salt sea back into drinkable fresh water? The fairy tale does not say. The fairy tale is obscure and opaque about how to remedy the tragedy of the salt grinder, how to turn it off, to stop it from producing salt in toxic amounts.

The tale was composed no later than the 1400s, before Carl Jung, before hypnosism before inner child work. These were the start of reliable methods to communicate directly with our inner salt grinder.

Inner child work empowers us to find and reprogram an errant salt grinder. It "lives" at the bottom of the ocean; so, time and effort are required to get down there.

The magic words required are: Acknowledgement, compassion, kindness, apology, self-forgiveness and re-negotiation.

To change the behavior of a rogue salt grinder, you have to GO DOWN INTO THE SEA, far down deep. Depending on the depth, this requires some courage. Deep sea diving requires some technique. Prepare before you dive.

Afraid of deep-sea-diving? The more you do it, the more familiar it becomes; your confidence increases. It becomes ordinary.

You're simply visiting parts of your psyche with much less choice than you are used to consciously, from the neck-up.

Your salt grinder is part of the human operating system. This is not safe, comfortable nor familiar. As a first-timer, this environment inevitably feels FOREIGN. James Cameron's movie, The Abyss is perhaps the best imagery we have of this journey, leading to a happy ending.

The deeper you go into your unconscious, the lower the frequency, towards Delta. You find more and more primitive thinking, less and less awareness choice exists. The deeper you go, the further away from "choice" you get. You bring choice to them; you bring a candle to your own darkness. The deeper part of our unconscious is far away from free choice. It does not understand and cannot make choices. You bring awareness and choice to these parts.

What do our unconscious parts know? They know rhythm and repetition (etheric), like a plant. This gives their current behavior-expression tremendous inertia and momentum.

What do they want down there? Primarily they want to continue doing what they are doing. The words "boredom," "new," "novelty" are not in their vocabulary any more than a plant becomes bored making new leaves or your blood gets bored circulating in your body.

Secondarily, they want to be released from carrying burdens no longer necessary for them to carry.

PTSD is exactly like this. The parts of us who do not know the worst is over can cycle thru old trauma pictures infinitely, like a needle stuck on a cracked record, in a never-ending manner, until someone can reach down and in to this part, who is perceived as safe and trustworthy to our Habit Body, who speaks to it relevantly: "The worst is over; you can relax now."

This is wisdom from one version of Emotional First Aid. It works for adults, kids, sub- and unconscious parts, anyone suffering.

The "Hobbit" in our "habits"

To point out the obvious, "hobbits" are called "hobbits" because they represent our "habits" and our practiced "comfort zones." Hobbits dislike change; they prefer to keep doing the same old comfortable routines they have done—forever. Dramatic tension forms when comfort-loving Hobbits are urged to leave their comfortable shire and go on a dangerous, unpredictable quest.

In this sense your own child within is like a "hobbit." Conscious Waking Self? That's Gandalf.

Chapter 6

Four Anatomies of our Habit Body

A) Habit Body in Three Selves terms

Functional equivalencies to "basic self" from the conscious self point of view

Enteric Habits, cerebral habits

B) Sleeping <=> dreaming <=> waking, the Iceberg model, Intelligences and Habits on three levels

C) Gestalt version: rhythms of contact - withdrawal

D) PACME (95%) Soul and Above (5%)

To switch metaphors, the top levels of our Habit Body are only dimly visible to us like the portion of an iceberg just below sea level.

A) Habit Body in Three Selves terms

This topic is taken up at length in two books:

You Have Three Selves; Simply the clearest model of the whole-person; Orientation, 2nd edition; and,

Holistic Neurology, Our Two Nervous Systems, Head-spine and enteric (gut) brains, Neurology for purposes of personal growth, Physiological basis for Self-esteem and Self-concept.

A brief version is the Three Selves acknowledges the reality of each person's own Higher Guidance. This is not Jesus, not Buddha; this is whatever Higher Guidance you subscribe to, individually determined. The home frequency of an individual's Higher Guidance varies considerably person to person.

Our two lower selves are Conscious Waking Self and our Child Within. Our Inner Child especially goes by 22 or more names, see a later chapter.

Our two lower selves have useful general physical locations. Conscious Self is our function of rational Feeling-Thinking. We primarily access this function in our neck-up.

Our Child Within (Habit Body) is our function of facilitating learning and storing learned behaviors on multiple levels of intelligence. We primarily access this function from our neck-down.

While lack of inner-cooperation between these two lower selves remains the biggest unresolved karma on Earth at this time (John-Roger), it is the destiny of these two to connect, communicate, collaborate and negotiate practical choices here in the human experience. Hence the big emphasis now, for those wishing to grow, to find and practice at least one method of healthy self-connection on a regular basis.

B) sleeping <=> dreaming <=> waking

Waking: thinking, choosing, deciding, initiating action.

Dreaming: daydreaming, feelings in general, liking, disliking and ambition in particular

Sleeping: peristaltic and metabolic activity, eye blinking and other reflexes.

Another 1919 Rudolf Steiner model. He gave this to his first Waldorf teachers so they could better understand how children and adults function on at least three levels while awake.

As Rudolf Steiner suggests:

some of our behavior is sleeping.

some of our behavior is dreaming, and

some of our behavior is waking.

RS suggests our human psyche is spread out over a range, over a continuum of frequency, a range of tempos.

Sleeping-dreaming-waking suggests how only about one-third of our life is spent in the "clear light of day" (RS) of waking conscious choice.

Two-thirds or more of our waking behavior is governed by habitual, or mostly-habitual responses, in the frequencies of dreaming and sleeping. Not surprisingly, the home of our reactivity.

Let's agree there are no fourth states of consciousness we have left out; let's agree sleeping-dreaming-waking covers both ends and every frequency in between, in the human psyche.

The vast majority of our behaviors and habits fall into these categories:

Sleeping-unconscious habits ~ our breathing pattern, our walking pattern, cell division (building healthy vs. Unhealthy new cells).

Dreaming-subconscious habits ~ speech patterns and dialects, self-talk patterns, daydreaming patterns.

Conscious habits ~ How we handle money, relate with children, pay the bills, decide what to do for fun.

W<=>D<=>S is a two way street

WDS is not static. It's a two way street.

In the direction towards higher frequency intelligences, towards wakefulness, Sleeping => dreaming => waking is the upswing towards making a decision, making a plan, connecting with others (or not), taking action.

In the direction towards lower frequency intelligences, this is the classic direction of falling asleep at night, allowing the intelligence of sleep to nurture, repair and rebuild our physical vehicle.

Other applications of WDS

RS suggested the three stages were also evident in human physiology. He said some organs are very awake (brain, eye, mouth). Other organs are dreaming (blood, skin, stomach, liver). Still other organs are sleeping (small intestine, bones, kidneys).

Sleeping => Dreaming => Waking

Imitative thinking => Taking on authority thinking => Independent thinking

An extended version of how this connects with leading children to healthy independent-critical thinking, for parents and educators, exists in Eugene Schwartz's book, *Millennial Child*, Transforming Education in the 21st Century (1999).

WDS in the light of Multiple Intelligences 2.0

From the viewpoint of Multiple Intelligences 2.0, "sleeping, dreaming, waking" is a continuum of wakefulness, from 'completely awake' to 'not consciously awake at all yet still functioning intelligently.'

Our Sleeping Intelligence is relatively inert, it's functions are very fixed and resistant to change.

Our Dreaming Intelligence is more active, primarily active in the realm of feeling. Physical children three years or younger have this as their primary waking intelligence of these three. Our inner child and Nature Spirits have Feeling as their primary intelligence. Feeling in humans is partly clear, partly unclear, not yet clear enuf to write essays and do pre-algebra.

Our Waking Intelligence is clear enuf to write essays and apply itself to pre-algebra; and with significant effort, beyond. Waking Intelligence is logical, linear and sequential.

That only ONE of these three Intelligences is the default connotation of the word "thinking" in English is part of the newness of our Sherlock Holmesian ability.   Rudolf Steiner said it's only been around since 1450, so it's the new kind on the block, still wet behind the ears, just beginning to integrate itself into any greater whole, since the mid-1960s, in some circles.

C) Gestalt Cycle: rhythm of contact~withdrawal

Learners gathered around Fritz Perls in the early 1970s worked out a visual to diagram a phenomena they observed repeatedly. They visualized contract~withdrawal as a regular wave form.

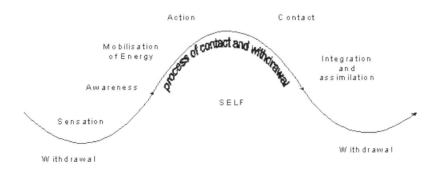

Habit Body 2nd ed ~ 85

bottom of the wave is habits taking over completely, sleeping-unconscious.

Notice the top of the wave is labeled action in the world and contact with other people. The bottom of the wave is labeled withdrawal and alone time.

It's a cycle, a rhythm of contact~withdrawal, contact~withdrawal. As long as each of us arrives fully at taking effective action in the world, connect with people; and, takes time for quality alone time, self-connection, then personal balance is sustainable.

Figure 1. The Gestalt Cycle: One Complete Gestalt (after Clarkson, 1989, p.29)

at all of growing our hair--yet someone is doing this and quite well.

Dreaming creativity ~ we are dimly aware of our dreams which may verge on wakeful participation. We are dimly aware of some aspects of digesting our food. We are somewhat aware of what happened in our childhood. We also receive hunches, guidance and intuition and we don't know for sure where these come from.

Waking creativity ~ we are fully awake and aware of reading this sentence now. We are fully awake and aware in choosing to do a random act of kindness, to write a letter, to pay the water bill. We are fully awake and aware in making choices generally. This is by design.

DYSfunctional habits on three levels

Our undesirable habits and unresolved disturbances are patterned the same way as our good habits:

waking <=> dreaming <=> sleeping

Why? Because every unwanted habit was still learned thru repetition just as every good habit was learned.

Conscious disturbances ~ things we know are disturbed and why they are disturbed: scraped knee, parking ticket, gaps between goals and reality.

Subconscious disturbances ~ uncomfortable feelings, vague sensing of disturbance; for example, unresolved childhood issues in adulthood.

Unconscious disturbances ~ Hidden, cloaked, disguised issues unknown to the rational mind. This is where most unresolved issues from prior existences are found.

Growth is a process of waking up, taking action to redirect old habits on any level: physical, imaginal, emotional, mental or unconscious.

In Inner Family + Inner Court; The Four Archetypes of Our Gut and Head, we show how all of our habits are conditioned by preferences.

Behavior = reactivity > preferences > habits > role playing > personality > destiny

D) Spiritual Geography 101, PACME

Q: Is there any way I can inventory my own personal habits?

A: Yes. You can inventory them by category using PACME.

Spiritual Geography comes from Light & Sound spiritual groups. All of them seem to subscribe to a very similar scheme of Creation below, Soul &

Above above in frequency, you as soul in Creation wherever your spiritual center of gravity happens to be at the moment.

This is not my idea and not a new idea. Significant literature has existed since 1850 and perhaps as far back as the 1400s with Guru Nanak.

According to John-Roger and everyone I can find on this topic, the "lay of the land" here in conditioned Creation, can be sketched as Physical Astral, Causal, Mental and Etheric (PACME). PACME uses the terms of Theosophy.

In my words, the human being is a microcosm in a macrocosm. The macrocosm of Spirit is organized in natural domains: physical, imaginative (astral), emotional (causal), mental and unconscious memories. We have habits on all these levels.

We have physical habits: posture, breathing pattern, reflexes such as eye-blinking and peristalsis, how we use a shovel, ride a bicycle, tie a knot in a necktie.

We have imaginal habits: what we fantasize about, patterns of daydreaming, patterns of expectation, patterns of liking and disliking people, places and things. Also patterns of ambition and revenge.

We have emotional habits: habits of over- and under-participation with people and commitments. Patterns of over-giving, under-giving and withholding.

We have mental habits: Most mental habits we call beliefs. These include cherished beliefs, good and bad; "things my grandmother used to tell me;" faulty and obsolete allegiances. When mind chatter is self-talk about liking and disliking, that's imaginal. Beliefs are habits, habits in the mental realm. Since the early 1990s, several modalities of muscle testing have enabled people to make great strides identifying, locating and clearing dysfunctional and faulty beliefs, Psych-K, Theta Healing and EFT.

We have mythological and mysterious habits: favorite memories; role models, models of what NOT to do, pet fears, unknown and mysterious habits on all above levels.

On each level, our workable habits keep us comfortable (comfort zone).

On each level, our unworkable habits become our "issues."

Growth is upgrading our habits on any level.

Having a comfort zone on each level PACME, our Habit Body is pretty interesting to work with.

Spiritual Geography supports us realizing anything we wish to change in ourselves, is no more nor less, than changing the habits on the relevant levels. Some readers will know this paraphrase is a big part of NLP's message.

The above sketch of layered frequencies or octaves, could be taught to college freshmen. If encountering PACME+Soul and Above gives you a sigh of relief, you are not alone. It's similar to finding a map and diagram of a giant indoor mall if you are lost and need the bathroom.

Thumbnail maps of the human psyche are especially useful for personal-spiritual growth because we are so often traversing ground new to us consciously. Maps are not the terrain but they give a sketch of what the terrain might be like. Conventional mainstream culture has no approved maps of the entire human psyche at all, so finding a good map of consciousness can be quite nice.

In the early 1970s a certain experiential meditation was popular and used in many learning settings. It goes like this.

Close your eyes. Quiet your pictures of what you like and dislike. Now quiet your feelings about what you love and hate. Now quiet your mind. Now quiet your memories. Okay, now. Who's doing that?

The One doing the quieting—however well or poorly—is your soul, the immortal-eternal spark in you, in all sentient beings.

Full discussion of PACME is in a 99 cent booklet, *You have FIVE bodies PACME; Spiritual Geography 101* (99 cents)

https://www.amazon.com/bodies-Spiritual-Geography-Practices-Medicine-ebook/dp/B007SIEC3S/ref=sr_1_1?ie=UTF8&qid=1476587865&sr=8-1&keywords=You+have+FIVE+bodies+PACME%3B+Spiritual+Geography+101

Here we assume beginning familiarity with the terms used in the above.

We have habits in our four invisible bodies, ACME.

For those familiar with aura studies, PACME can also be visually represented as concentric circles.

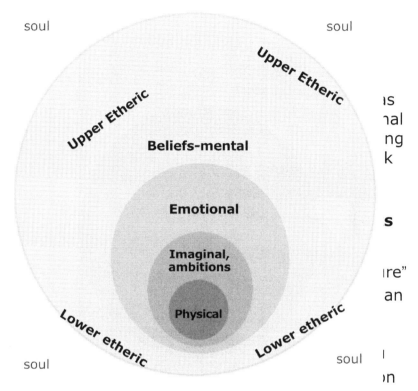

soul   soul

Upper Etheric

Upper Etheric

Upper Etheric

Beliefs-mental

Emotional

Imaginal, ambitions

Physical

Lower etheric

Lower etheric

soul   soul

ıs

ıal

ng

k

s

ıre"

an

I

ın

one of his Prairie Home Companion radio broadcasts.

What do we learn "is so" by age 12? The written and unwritten rules of our local culture. Culture IS the written and unwritten rules you grow up with. That's why Garrison's Lake Woebegone news reports are funny to us. Listeners hear the gap between the written--and unwritten rules--of the sub-culture of Lake Woebegone and our mainstream culture.

This is why K-12 education is a cultural battleground. K-12 is where culture is formed, where culture wars are won or lost.

What we call culture, what we call human nature, are not more nor less than big collection baskets of habits.

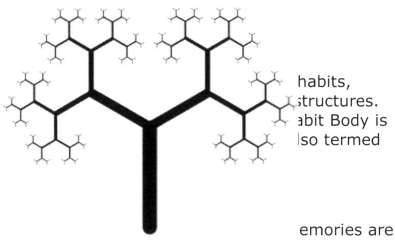 habits,
structures.
abit Body is
lso termed

emories are
unconscious habits.

Notice at the depth of the point directly above, left brain language is no longer useful nor applicable.

If you grasp how beliefs are mental habits, formed thru repetition, it won't surprise you to hear, memories are mostly unconscious habits, learned thru repetition too. As with everything in our unconscious, both beliefs and memories are "out of sight, out of mind," unless and until, we need them, recall them or something triggers them and wakes them to conscious attention.

It will help visual readers to imagine beliefs and memories as coming from "far away" inside you. This is true in a frequency sense. Indeed memories are so deep in our unconscious, that traveling to meet the deepest ones face to face, can take a lifetime. Our Habit Librarian equates "change of frequency" with "distance."

NLP taught us memories-as-habits are composed of stored memory percepts. That's all any memory is, a set of associated sensory percepts. Most of these are felt-sense (kinesthetic) but sound, color and taste images can accompany felt-sense memories. In how they are composed, no memory is any more or less real than any other habit. They are each and all collections of associated sense perceptions. As NLP taught us, if you release the unresolved charge on all the associated sense memories, you release the memory.

Terms for intensity of a habit

A habit is a thought form repeated so it expands and gains enuf energy to penetrate down into the emotions and pre-physical body.

An addiction is a habit repeated, a more entrenched and ingrained habit.

An obsession is a repeated addiction.

In the positive, I encourage you to have as many positive, healthy obsessions as workable for you today.

John-Roger on "inner-cooperation"

J-R suggested "lack of inner cooperation is the biggest problem on the planet" (pretty accurate paraphrase I think). This idea is reflected in the numerology J-R used for a period; where, the vast majority of individuals have the number "2," in their Life Plan numerology. Late in his use of numerology in Light Studies, he expanded this to nine levels of cooperation, all the ways he could list, of how we cooperate with Self, Others, World God.

"Two" in numerology classically represents "inner cooperation," cooperation, collaboration, harmony, within one single individual. That is, between gut brain and head brain, between Conscious Waking Self and the Habit Body, the Child Within. "4" then represents cooperation, collaboration, harmony between two persons.

This is why "4" is the "marriage number" in numerology.

"6" then is cooperation, collaboration, harmony among three or more.

"8" is "material success" cooperation, collaboration, harmony on a larger scale.

"10" is cooperation, collaboration, harmony with Spirit.

"12" is even masterful and Queenly cooperation, collaboration, harmony in social relations.

"22" Is Master Magician, where the focus is building, sustaining and growing local community, how to apportion resources for the highest good for all concerned.

Early even numbers represent variations of "cooperation" starting with inner-cooperation "2."

We see examples of healthy inner-cooperation primarily in two places:

- Inner Child work of all kinds, and

- Self-muscle-testing of all kinds (arm-length-testing now preferred).

What does inner cooperation look like?

Inner cooperation can now be defined as cooperation between the C/s and basic self. Healthy cooperation inside your psyche, among your Three Selves, is not automatic, not an automatic given.

A high degree of cooperation between our Three Selves is not automatic, not a given. How do most people begin experimenting and practicing? Inner Child work and self-connection methods of every kind, including yoga, meditation, gratitude journal. Too boring for you? A Skill Ladder of Self-connection Methods exists. How high can you climb?

If you practice self-connection, connection between Conscious Self and Habit Body, you will improve. The only wrong way to try is not to try at all. Over time, a more loving quality begins appearing. Go towards it.

Q: Why is all this growth-stuff about going inside? Can I do extreme sports as my form of self-connection?

A: John-Roger was asked this. His response was people who embrace extreme sports and dangerous sports are indeed looking for a peak experience of integration, wholeness. Perhaps they even use "God" to describe what they aspire to.

Risking your life is one way to attempt self-connection. How sustainable this is for how many people, always seems to be very low. I'm reminded of a friend in a spiritual group who had a past life reading she thought was accurate. My friend was told she died several times in Tibet flying home-made hang gliders between the steep and cold mountains. She understood the thrill of this. She also understood she was back here on Earth again, so hang-gliding was no ultimate answer for her as an immortal soul.

Somehow, sooner or later, for all of us, we face a paradox: the greatest expansions possible in Feeling and Consciousness are only available by going inside. Still working on this paradox myself too.

The seemingly inevitable signpost, "The Kingdom of Heaven in within" seems to be the 'revenge of the Introverts on an Extraverted world.'

Chapter 7

Habits form around our five universal needs

We are born with five universal needs

I have special loving for William Glasser, all his innovations. They culminate for me in two books, *Choice Theory, A New Psychology of Personal Freedom*; and, *Getting Together and Staying Together: Solving the Mystery of Marriage*

Paperback – 2000

Copies: http://www.allbookstores.com/

Reviews: https://www.amazon.com/Getting-Together-Staying-Solving-Marriage/dp/006095633X/ref=sr_1_1?s=books&ie=UTF8&qid=1471915352&sr=1-1&keywords=glasser+staying+together

Some readers will know Glasser from Reality Therapy (1969). In 1996 Glasser drastically changed his approach, integrating Choice Theory into Reality Therapy (Corey, sixth ed p. 230 footnote).

survival   love-belonging   power   freedom   fun

The five needs in Glasser's version can use some expansion:

Survival	needs, not wants	s
Love and Belonging	intimacy, closeness, connection	of
Power	influence with your peers	
Freedom	set your own goals, control your own time	٦y
Fun	celebration, distraction and novelty	

met and fulfilled. However, each of us prioritizes the five needs according to individual preference.

Glasser says it's easy to identify how you rate and prioritize the five needs, which is highest for you, which are secondary, and so on. An arbitrary sample:

For comparing needs between two people, you need two profiles to compare. On your own paper, please assign a value to each need on a five point scale.

What is your own personal "needs profile"? The easy way to do this is to guess at your strongest need. then guess at your weakest need. Fill in the others as you think fit. Sleep on it. See if you like the order the next day. Once your order is stable for three days in a row, that's a snapshot of your Needs Profile now.

Q: Can I do this for clients?

A: If you wish to power-trip clients, sure do it FOT them. If you wish to empower a client, I would ONLY do this WITH them in person. Encourage them to self-evaluate. This helps them believe the numbers can change over time.

If you take this up, you will quickly learn how different people prioritize the same needs differently. Glasser has much discussion about who gets along with who, for which purpose—like relationships—according to how each partner prioritizes needs.

The need for which you have the most number of workable habits, is likely to be where you experience the most success. The need where you have the fewest number of working habits and routines, is likely a weak area in your life.

Want to get along with children? Remember these five words. Having a problem teaching students or with adult subordinates? Group process becomes dysfunctional when one or more of these needs is not getting met according to participants.

Diagram the priority of your needs now

Our individual Needs Profile offers obvious therapeutic direction for each of us. We all want each of our five needs met and fulfilled. However, each of us prioritizes these needs according to our personal preferences.

Glasser says it's easy to identify how you rate and prioritize the five needs, which is highest for you, which are secondary, and so on.

For more precision—and for comparing needs between two people--Glasser suggests assigning value to each need on a five point scale:

These numbers above are my own personal "needs profile." What is your needs profile?:

Q: I like this and I wonder if these five needs could be made more elegant?

A: Me too. The book *Inner Family + Inner Court; The Four Archetypes of Our Gut and Head* discusses how Glasser's five needs distribute themselves gracefully over the four archetypal figures of the Inner Court.

After much practice with Glasser's ideas, I think clearer to claim "In English humans have Five Universal Needs."

For beginners and the public, stick with Glasser's five needs. Ready for a bigger picture? The bigger, language-neutral picture is Four Archetypal needs.

Chapter 8

Habits as "drama"

In watching a play in a theater, without different habit patterns, how would you know one actor from another? In theater and drama especially, characters are defined by how they react.

Reactive patterns are the basis of most drama. In fact the reaction "revenge" is so common in movies, about 50% of all movies would be wiped out or never made if "revenge" had to be removed from character motivation. "Revenge" is hundreds of times more common in fiction than in real life. Much of this is lazy storytelling, lazy screenwriting. Easy to build a story around revenge. More challenging to build a story around character growth and development.

If we allow drama in our life, we tend to play the part of victim, perpetrator or rescuer. Yes, you can change roles, go back and forth. In families of origin where drama is valued, everyone "has to" play one or more of these roles. Without patterns of reacting, how would we know one brother from another, one sister from another?

Habit Body as Drama Body

Our Habit Body can be reframed as our 'Drama Body.' Your Drama Body is the sum of all your habits keeping you in drama, drama with your self, drama with other people, drama with the world, drama with God and authorities over you.

'Habit Body' is a positive frame: towards more healthy habits.

'Drama Body' is an away, negative frame: let's reduce drama, trauma, upset and disturbance.

Your Drama Inventory

What's your Drama Inventory? It's possible to make a pie chart graph of "drama," exploring your own Drama Profile in five frequencies:

Physical drama, health, lifestyle and living situation,

Imaginal drama, negative self-talk, gossip, blame, complaining,

Emotional drama, what pulls at your heart-strings? How do you know? Longing, yearning, devotion, sacrifice, martyrdom.

Mental drama, comparing, evaluating, judging in all forms, faulty beliefs and allegiances

Mythological drama, your role models, positive and negative. Faulty role-models, 'Old Testaments' we still worship in our unconscious. Scripts People Live, Redecision Therapy, Core Transformation.

Habits around roles of Victim, Persecutor, Rescuer

If we suffered in one of these roles, we may have habits (memories) around playing the Victim, playing the Persecutor and playing the Rescuer in the Karpman Drama Triangle in Reactivity Is Our Best Friend, New Directions in Holistic Brain Balance (Vol 3) or ask Mr. Google.

Addicted to trauma

Below is a somewhat confused exchange from a PTSD forum. It's the top-rated Google results for "addicted to drama:"

Ningamer: Has anyone felt like they were addicted to trauma or at least trauma related things?Sometimes I become so numb and emotionless, I'll trigger myself or wish trauma would happen again.

I guess it's because it makes me feel emotion. Being in pain seems to be better than feeling dead. I guess it just makes me feel alive. Maybe I'm just addicted to pain, both emotional and physical.

Manic11: Well, I seem to bring myself to watch movies about sexual abuse survivors and war victims, people who have dealt with traumas. These trigger me; and yet, I still want to watch things like that.

I believe it's because I grew up being abused. From when I was a baby up until very recent. It's what I'm used to. I can't grasp people who have not been abused... Fantastic if they escape--but it's like... that really happens? Are there really people who have parents who treat them well?

Abuse is what I'm used to. If I'm treated too well, it's almost scary. I'm not used to it. This may be why I bring myself back to watching those movies. It also makes me feel understood. I don't know... I hope this helps hun...

Ningamer: Yes that's exactly what I mean! I don't know what it's like to be healthy, and I don't even

know what I would consider healthy. I guess I'm
so used to unhealthy and trauma-related
behavior, I always end up falling back into.I found
an article
(http://healing.about.com/od/emotionalissues/a/p
tsd_jgazley.htm). It sums up what I'm talking
about:

Whenever a child feels abandonment from one or
both of their parents, they internalize the hurt.
The result is a feeling of not being good enough to
be loved, a feeling of shame. Even if parents are
relatively healthy and loving, a child can feel
tremendous abandonment if their parents get
divorced, if a parent is alcoholic, or if parents
simply work too much and not spend enough
quality time a child needs. This often leads to a
deep emotional belief in the child, they are
unlovable.Later, they might realize on a conscious
level they are loveable; and in turn, desire real
love. Consciously they look for healthy love; yet
subconsciously, they search out those people who
are incapable of showing real love. This is called a
repetition compulsion. This problem becomes
worse if the child has been physically,
emotionally, or sexually abused.They find true
love boring and yearn for people to treat them
poorly, which validates their feeling unlovable.
They often become addicted to these abusive
relationships. they feel they cannot live without
them. They become intensity junkies instead of

trying to experience true intimacy. Finding partners who cannot commit, is a variation on this theme.

The above is how many people process unhealthy addictions absent a Habit Body model and absent a more sophisticated Gestalt-TA understanding of dynamics in our unconscious.

Much of the missing language for the above can be found in, "Why We Pick the Mates We Do: Our Unconscious Matchmaker" (https://www.youtube.com/watch?v=gYNDo4teQ7 4) a video magazine I made which summarizes and improves a bit on the book by by TA-Gestalt expert, Anne Teachworth. (1997) *Why We Pick The Mates We Do*. Gestalt Institute Press. ISBN 1-889968-53-6

Trauma bonding

Trauma-bonding: when one person voices how they survived a past trauma, other individuals in the room, perk up and speak their own story of trauma or abuse. This is often an attempt to bond with the first speaker thru mutual past, negative experiences. It's possibly sympathy also. The bad news is unless both speakers get around to looking forward, trauma-bonding can be only backward-looking, focussed on the past, who you were in the past, when the abuse was suffered; instead of, supporting each other to identify and affirm new goals, identifications and new healthy boundaries.

Awfulizing and gossip

Awfulizing is a habit.

Awfulizing (noun) Refers to an irrational-dramatic thought pattern, characterized by overestimating the potential seriousness or negative consequences of events, situations, or perceived threats.

AWFULIZING: "A person who engages in awfulizing, is prone to predict the most catastrophic outcome in every circumstance" ~ PsychologyDictionary.com

Gossip is a habit, the mildest form of awfulizing and trauma bonding.

Chapter 9

Workable habits as "comfort zone"

Another name for a workable habit is "comfort zone." "Habits" and "comfort zones" are closely connected.

We have habits/comfort-zones physically, imaginally, emotional, mentally, and unconsciously (PACME).

Habits we come to rely on, we identify with. We can deepen our identification with habits and become dependent on them.

When "rocks our boat," challenges our comfort zone, our homeostasis, it's possible to become defensive and dig in, deepening identification more.

Each comfort zone is a bunch of habits

Take any comfort zones you have. Consider it's composed of a bunch of related habits. What daily routine are you most fond of?

Analyze the average person's comfort zone and what you find is only a bunch of habits, behaviors conditioned by personal preference and repetition.

Once set in motion, our Habit Body, like any good Hobbit, does its best to maintain, preserve, sustain and repeat it.

Our Habit Body per se is not into "improvement" much. It vaguely wants "to do better next time" (RS) but has no scheme for this or goal beyond what a three year old might have.

Our Habit Body is designed for pumping out routine behaviors moment to moment, so a baseline of comfort and predictability is sustained. Our Habit Body is not designed to initiate "makeovers" of any kind.

It may be so unhappy it dearly wants a "makeover;" however, without partnering with Conscious waking Self, nothing happens, nothing changes. Attempts at positive change are at best hit or miss.

Comfort Zones as Homeostasis

Temperature homeostasis for our physical body is often defined as 98.6 degrees. Homeostasis is not too hungry, not too thirsty, not too hot, not too cold. Not too much of anything, nor, too little of anything.

We all put effort into adjusting the pulleys and levers of our life aiming to keep as many comfort zones going as we can.

Wikipedia reminds us, "a person's personality can be described by his or her comfort zones." Our mental-emotional comfort zones approximate what we call 'my personality.'

If we had NO comfort zones, life wouldn't be worth living. A modicum of comfort zones is indispensable to happiness. The younger you are, the more this is true; because, a child has less ability to change its circumstances.

Comfort zones are homeostasis in our psyche, 'psychological homeostasis.'

Our mental-emotional comfort zone is all habits we like, those workable for us, comfortable for us. Within our comfort zones, we feel capable and confident.

Consider: The bigger our comfort zones on each level, PACME, the more capable-confident we feel. Conversely, the smaller and fewer our comfort

zones on each level, PACME, the less capable-
confident we feel.

This is why parents attempt to protect and
nurture children. Your child is building up their
healthy comfort zones, excellence requires
gentleness, expertise and consistency.

Generally we dislike others disturbing-interrupting
our comfort zone habits. We have language for
this, "upsetting the apple cart;" and, "rocking the
boat."

But what if our comfort zones take over and we
tolerate living only where we feel comfortable?

Most meaningful joke in the world

This is a joke illustrating comfort zones; I first
heard this from John-Roger:

One dark night a policeman is walking his beat
and comes across a drunk frantically searching for
something on the ground. The drunk is half
naked, wearing his shirt, jacket and hat but
missing his pants, shoes and socks. He is
scrambling around on his hands and knees, in the
circle of light under a street lamp.

The policeman looks on the ground in the light and can see there is nothing to be found there. "What are you looking for?"

"Well, Officer, I can't find my keys."

"Do you remember where you saw them last?" The drunk points across the street to a dark overgrown area of bushes.

"I lost them over there, Officer."

"Then why are you looking for them over here?"

"Well Officer—over here—the light's better."

Our familiar comfort zones are the "light" to Conscious Self, where we trust and believe things are safe, trustable and predictable. Our comfort zones are the most "lighted" places in our psyche.

The converse is also true. The further away and outside of our comfort zones, the more unsafe, untrustworthy and unpredictable life is.

An immature—or drunk—individual wishes to find all his or her answers to Life's problems only within our cozy, warm little psychic nest. We don't wanna leave the nest. We don' wanna go out into the cold and dark, where many problems need to be solved, outside the sameness of a life of comfort.

This is how our child within, our Habit Body thinks.

If we are looking for something not present, it's for darn sure NOT nearby, within arm's reach, NOT in our comfort zones, no matter how much we wish it weren't so.

The drunk wants his solution to be inside his lighted zone, where he can find things easily. He's not feeling strong enuf to put on shoes, coat, hat, gloves and go out into the dark bushes where his keys wait for him.

The pattern of wanting our solutions to be where they are easy to find, occurs when our comfort zones overpower our willingness to learn and transform in the direction of our goals and projects. The human experience invites us to S-T-R-E-T-C-H, to go beyond our comfy places, to consider which reasonable risks are worth taking.

In the 1980s, NLP put it this way: If you don't like the results you are getting, you want different results; then, you have to change your behavior. Keep changing it until the results you want begin to appear. Do more of those habits. Anyone wishing different results today and in the future, must change from how you behaved yesterday.

What happens is we often give up on our healthy goals before we have changed-expanded our behavior sufficiently beyond what felt comfortable and familiar yesterday.

"You receive not because ye ask not"

A big job Conscious Self has is acknowledging and communicating with our Habit Body.

Why? No matter how much I learn, Conscious Waking Self never has 100% of the facts to make perfect decisions confidently. We're always making decisions, even big ones, on partial information. This is simply the nature of soul in Earthly experience.

Our basic self, our Habit Body knows quite a bit, but it is yin to our YANG. Like a two-year-old learning to talk, it does not say much unless you ASK her. For most people now, we can't learn what our Habit Body knows or wants unless and until we ASK. I have to ASK. Any conscious Self behaving like a Know It All, is preparing for a Humpty Dumpty fall. Having all the facts before we act is a faulty goal in more situations than we prefer.

When we know little, asking for assistance is not weak; it's proof of open-mindedness, flexible thinking, not being stuck. Playing Lone Ranger is good evidence we are stuck somewhere. Hence, the stereotype of lost men refusing to ask for directions.

Habits: the Garden of Eden metaphor

Paraphrased from Geoffrey Rose's When You Get to the End of Your Rope Let Go (X-Libris, 2001).

We have good habits:

- spending daily quality time with our children,

- going to the dentist every six months

- eating healthy,

- saying, "Please" and, "Thank you,"

We have lousy habits:

- lousy posture,

- gossip,

- getting angry in traffic.

And some habits are neutral:

- walk the dog,

- take out the trash,

- chew food,

- watch the news.

Because habits are planted by intention, take root in the basic self and grow thru repetition, we can view our habits as our own little Garden of Eden.

In springtime (youth) our Garden of Eden looks green and great. Over time, (around 21) we begin seeing habits that once worked, that no longer work for us; like, never putting away the laundry--ever. Then the alert gardener goes to work weeding and pruning. = change your habits.

The skilled mature gardener has two aims in mind, to nurture desirable plants AND to remove unwanted growth and weeds. Wow, our garden has many kinds of growth. Some are valued flowers. Some are green and that's enuf. Some are weeds we will some day get around to pulling up by the roots.

We have valued talents and traits we love and that others love us for. Keep these lovely habits, like physical and spiritual exercise. These are worth nurturing and increasing. We have habits and behaviors serving us well but which are unspectacular. These don't draw attention and don't need changing now. We also have perennial weeds needing to be pulled up by the roots once and for all. No more just cutting them off at "see level."

Personal growth can be viewed as nurturing the plants we do want AND removing growth no longer appropriate to our goals and alignment. It's served its purpose. Gardeners get busy and pull as many weeds as possible in the time available. Start with the biggest ones Gardening is fun for all ages.

Why don't more people garden? Why do we delay and by default, hang on to weeds that need pulling up? Hmmm the basic self grew all these plants, every one. If we grew it, we tend to have a vested interest in it, an attachment. We don't wish to see our creation destroyed.

Find more and different Garden of Eden and plant language for habits in Geoffrey Rose's When You

Get to the End of Your Rope Let Go (X-Libris, 2001).

Outgrowing old comfort zones

It's Natural and healthy for us to outgrow old comfort zones.

Taken altogether, our comfort zones are the sum of all habits we like and feel comfortable with. Within these comfortable habits, we feel supported, capable and confident (sound like any Hobbits you know?)

Generally the bigger our comfort zone, the more competent and confident we feel. In people with healthy comfort zones, you see an attractive ease and expansiveness.

We don't require a huge comfort zone in order to grow. All we need is adequate and sufficient comfort; and, some extra good feeling enabling us to take reasonable risks.

The mechanism of dilemma and stuckness

The phenomena of "having too much to lose" operates even more strongly with groups of people. Hence the old parable, the difficulty of putting new wine in old wine skins.

The dilemma about giving up unhealthy choices can be seen on a macro level in the dilemma about war and militarism, another basket of habits.

Militarism, using force against force in the present world situation, rarely works well. Yet the collective military-industrial-congressional complex does not feel able to give up using force against force.

Militarism is stimulating on so many levels, to give it up for peace and diplomacy, for few jobs making bombs and planes to fly them, a lowered level of sensory stimulation, seems like too much of a sacrifice.

For peace to become attractive to an individual, peace has to be high on their scale of values. With this in place, then, healthy leadership can coordinate group movement towards greater benefits for the majority.

A surplus of self-esteem has to be present in order to risk new behavior. Choosing change requires emotional capital to make change. A mood of expansion is the pre-requisite to try new things.

The basic self has to feel supported from outside or inside, be in a mood of expansion towards proposed change. Without feeling expansive, it's likely to hold on to what it had yesterday.

What it takes to take risks

We require adequate and sufficient comfort to feel good enuf to risk new behavior, try a new action. People don't risk and grow, try new things, unless they feel relatively good about themselves. Happy people take more risks than most depressed people.

Taking a risk is an investment, is a gamble. People don't take risks unless they have some extra good feeling about themselves to gamble with.

Comfort zones as 'unconscious inertia'

Like Hobbits, our Habit Body wants to do the same thing next year as it did last year. In this, our Habit Body tends towards inertia, not towards change nor healthy risking.

Habits and comfort zones have inertia. Wikipedia: "a person who has established a comfort zone in a particular part of his or her life, will tend to stay in their zone without stepping outside of it."

Our mind, emotions and unconscious are all subject to inertia.

A Habit Body makes more clear why the one thing human beings do better than anything else is making the same mistake over and over and over again.

Chapter 10

Our unexamined habits become our illnesses

Habits needing change come to conscious attention primarily when they get in our way:

- This really doesn't work for me any more,

- This isn't me anymore,

- I feel blocked here,

- I'd like to change this.

If you hear yourself saying any of these, somebody inside is ready for a change.

Willingness to change usually involves waking up to suffering we no longer wish to put up with:

"I know this is a problem for me. This is something I need to work on." Eventually: "I am sick and tired of being sick and tired and I'm not going to take it any more!" Change is now very likely.

Acutely depressed people have so little comfort zone to lose, big risks, even unhealthy risks, attract them. They may think, "What have I got to lose?"

Our ego protects us from everything feared– usefully or not.

Denial keeps us from needed changing

Denial is an expression of willfulness. Most people believe "honesty is the best policy"—except with themselves. Denial leads directly to feeling stuck-- and denying we are stuck. If a habit does not work, sooner or later you will get around to changing it.

Smoking cigarettes is the classic example of a habit which left unexamined leads to lung cancer, etc.

In 2017 we can mention the habit of eating unrestricted sugar and carbs, at any age, leads to diabetes.

"Physical illness are our modern gods"

Carl Jung once suggested, "physical illnesses are the modern gods." The quote source still eludes me. We do have:

Only in exceptional cases are somatic stimuli the determining causative factor in a physical symptom. Usually physical symptoms devolve completely from . . . disturbed unconscious expression. ...

Revised from "General Aspects of Dream Psychology"(1916). In CW 8: The Structure and Dynamics of the Psyche. P. 502

... countless physical illnesses are tainted and complicated with psychic material to an unsuspected degree ... ~ In CW4: Freud and Psychoanalysis. P.578

https://archive.org/stream/MemoriesDreamsRefle ctionsCarlJung/Carl%20Jung%20Quotations%20s ourced%20final_djvu.txt

Jung was unable to follow up on this, even to connect the "shadow" directly with physical illness, beyond his correct intuition of their connection. Nor can I find any follow-up from Jung on this.

Carl Jung and Rudolf Steiner

Freud, Jung and Steiner were all born in Switzerland or Austria and all within 19 years of each other.

Jung's wife tried to arrange for Carl to meet his contemporary Rudolf Steiner, when Steiner was nearby on his lecture tours. Carl refused repeatedly. What if the two had met? Jung would likely have been exposed to an early version of the Spiritual Geography-Habit Body model of how illness forms.

Using the PACME model, it's more clear how negativity in a higher frequency level must "downshift" before it can manifest here in the physical-material world, in our body.

The Habit Body model tells us all habits are primarily invisible, visible only as behavior.

This means our bad habits are also primarily invisible—at least at first.

Invisible negativity must "rehearse" over and over to gather sufficient strength to manifest all the way down and out in the physical-material dimension.

This path into manifestation may sound familiar; it's not unique.

We as souls in the human experience arrive thru the birth canal the exact same way. Metaphysics tells us it takes great strength to move an idea from the invisible world out into the visible world of 3D matter.

John-Roger has said only the strong souls make it here into physical baby bodies. Look back on your own life. How much courage was required for you to survive all the insults, injustices and deficiencies of your younger years? For most of us, we can count many obstacles in a course of obstacles, we had to successfully navigate to be here today. You too?

Physical illness is no different. Nothing inward becomes physically present unless-until it practices, rehearses, repeats until it has the strength to manifest outwardly. No more and no less.

I wish not to go so far to declare our illnesses a heroic act. However, if you, as the Play Director, the Play Producer, don't think the play the actors are rehearsing will be good nor successful, why don't you call it quits on rehearsals and cut your losses?

This updates and modernizes many metaphysical teachings.

Let's turn it around: For Success to manifest physically, it too must exist in our inner ACME worlds first before it can manifest outwardly here in the 3D world. This paraphrases the workable part of the Law of Attraction.

Illness must be gradually born into the physical, just like everything else in 3D.

We are not thinking our clearest when we imagine our problems are primarily or exclusively physical-material. 10% physical, 5% physical is the clear thought here.

Every phenomena in 3D--including any physical illness--has to have an imaginal, emotional, mental and unconscious existence prior to becoming present here in 3D matter.

This is not my idea; it's simply part of the design specs of physical Creation.

Everything here in 3D devolves from above, picking up substance as it moves down, until it can make its appearance on the "stage" of 3D materiality.

If each illness did NOT have an Imaginal Emotional, Mental and Mythological "body" above it (ACME), it could not be present physically. It would be like a stage role with scripted lines but no actor to speak them or play the part on stage.

A: Okay I got a disease I don't want. Where are the invisible habits causing it?

A: This is a worthwhile question, worth asking often.

Each person is somewhat unique in how their habits were formed and are arranged. We know for sure your physical disease can in large measure be tracked back to habits which are imaginal, emotional, mental and unconscious (ACME). They had to be there before they could become physical (P).

We know the physical aspect of your dis-ease must have precipitated from your higher frequency invisible bodies.

Another metaphor for how things manifest in the physical, is 'stepping down a staircase of frequencies' towards an appearance, at last, on the stage of the physical world. A physical body is the lowest, most outer and slowest of all levels of Creation in the human experience.

The shadow in pop culture fiction

In terms of fictional characters, the Shadow Archetype is the part of a personality embodying everything a character, called the 'Self', doesn't like about themselves, the aspects of themself they deny and project out onto others.

To show this internal duality dramatically to an audience, we need to embody it in some form. In pop culture, we call some of these embodiments:

Classic Villain

Enemy Within

Enemy Without

Evil Counterpart

Evil Twin

Jekyll & Hyde

... On occasion when the two are gender/orientation compatible, the hero might find their counterpart intriguing, and end up dating the shadow. This rarely ends well [in pop culture fiction]...

A common trope involves the Self accepting their own Shadow, acknowledging, coming to terms with their flaws. Sometimes given opportunity, the Hero refuses to kill his evil Shadow, refuses to fight it.

In Enemy Within, Enemy Without, and Evil Twin situations, the Self and Shadow sometimes even merge towards the end for an endgame team-up, further emphasizing the symbolism. ...

Reduced from
http://tvtropes.org/pmwiki/pmwiki.php/Main/Sha
dowArchetype

The "psychological shadow"

In the mid-late 1800s, the shadow, the double, the doppelganger, was always negative. Readers familiar with how recent the concept of "childhood" is, will know the redeeming of the psychological shadow parallels exactly rising awareness and attention paid to children and effective parenting skills.

An individual's positive self-concept is composed of behaviors and memories judged as "positive." Our Shadow is everything in contrast. It "holds" all behaviors and memories we do NOT identify with, every aspect of ourself we judge as negative. See also, "Picture of Dorian Gray" motif.

Habit Body 2nd ed ~ 135

Jung wrote, "the less it is embodied in the individual's conscious life, the blacker and denser [the shadow] is ~ Wikipedia

The completely negative shadow began evolving towards the positive with Carl Jung (primarily in the 1940s?) "in Jungian psychology, the Shadow Archetype includes positive as well as negative things, anything suppressed or denied in the personality" ~ http://tvtropes.org

Due to the positive effects of Freudian psychoanalysis; and, Jungian ideas, in the 1940s, in New York City especially, the first primitive, rudimentary pop-culture "redemption" of the psychological shadow appeared: the Shadow radio hero. The shadow remains "of the dark," yet can align with the forces of good.

The next positive evolution was evident in the 1970s when the psychological shadow was "upgraded" to the Inner Child metaphor. This became a mainstream topic, furthered by John Bradshaw in the 1980s.

The new holistic-humanistic view of the Child Within was much more forgiving. This begins the whole related meme of the "Nurturing Parent."

In getting our meme history straight, "Stern Father" was the predominant parenting paradigm for several thousands years, East and West, up to WW II. After WW II the "Stern Father" paradigm began slowly to erode; by the 1970s, the "Stern Father" paradigm was seriously eroded.

It was replaced in holistic-humanistic-liberal circles with the more positive "Nurturing Parent" paradigm. The holistic-humanistic Inner child of the 1970s and 1980s is a redemptive motif. The Child Within could and should be talked with—not to; it should be educated, it should receive opportunities to improve behavior, it can be redeemed. We as Conscious Selves have this duty and obligation. So says the "Nurturing Parent" paradigm.

Yet in circles of discourse and conversation far removed from holistic-Humanistic Psychology, Stern Father was replaced with--nothing. What comes in to fill this vacuum? Consumerism, emptiness, nihilism, depression, chaos. See "Logan" movie (2017). The failed—still very attached to past glories mindset, Eric Idle calls the "Great White Male."

To review, the psychological shadow model began as a narrative device. It expanded into a psychological meme: everything negative in an individual. Over time, the psychological shadow evolved 'towards the light,' towards everything in an individual adult psyche of which the person is not fully conscious--good and bad. Redemption of children is the obligation of adults. Redemption of your own shadow is up to you. So says holistic-humanistic-liberal ideology, pointing us towards a Hero's Journey sooner or later.

In the post-2012 world the psychological shadow remains a widely used model in counseling, psychotherapy and Energy Medicine where it overlaps virtually 100% with the Inner Child.

Examples:

To know yourself, you must accept your dark side. To deal with others' dark sides, you must also know your dark side ~ Wikipedia

Merger with the shadow ~ According to Jung, the shadow sometimes overwhelms a person's actions; for example, when the conscious mind is shocked, confused, or paralyzed by indecision. 'A man possessed by his shadow is always standing in [the way of] his own [higher] light and falling into his own traps ... living below his own level'[20]. Hence, in "Dr Jckyll and Mr Hyde," 'it must be Dr. Jekyll, the conscious personality, who integrates the shadow ... and not vice versa. [Dr. Jekyll succumbs and] the conscious self becomes the slave of the autonomous shadow' [21] ~ Wikipedia

The most advanced post-modern psychotherapeutic interventions, such as:

- Solution-Focussed Brief Therapy (1990s),

- Some NLP methods (1970s-present),

- Rational Emotive Behavior Therapy (REBT), Cognitive Emotional Behavior Therapy (CEBT), et al. (primarily 1980s?),

- Energy Medicine methods incorporating the above with additional self-testing, meridian and energetic methods.

All of the above trend away from both earlier judgmental-negative frames on our psychological shadow; all of the above move towards more neutral framing, emphasizing client choice.

All of the above encourage witnessing undesirable behavior: uncovery. After discovery-uncovery, interventions can be initiated to redirect unwanted-undesirable habits-behaviors, initiating and establishing new, healthier habits-behaviors.

The above summarizes the leading edge of the most effective practices in client support and self healing since 1990.

Q: In the post-modern paradigm, is there a part of our psyche, a part of our Habit Body, where all our negative aspects live?

A: Emphatically no. The concept of a single repository of all which is bad and wrong with us— known and unknown—is a 19th century concept.

"Projection," blame and scapegoating

Our Child Archetype is subconscious and unconscious. Most people are unaware of its activity. Our Child Within is very capable of and prone to, project liking and disliking onto other people and things.

When our Child archetype projects personal inferiority, as a moral deficiency, onto another person, religious or ethnic group, we have scapegoating.

Once the 20th century idea of psychological projection became widespread in professional circles, it became clear the "evil doppelganger" motif is simply a childish wish that all our annoying bad habits and un-redeemed parts can be surgically removed and placed in another container, another person, a picture ("Picture of Dorian Gray"), our spouse, an ethic minority and other scapegoating tactics based on unexamined psychological projection.

As late as the 1960s lobotomies were considered a positive and progressive treatment for stubborn mental illness. Who thinks this now?

Q: How does our Habit Librarian organize negativity?

A: NEW Energy Anatomy suggests our Habit Librarian has very clear 3D spatial templates for where to store unwanted habits in our habit hologram.

Our Habit Librarian has the job of ordering arrangements of all habits, on all levels; including, habits we like and habits we dislike. How? It arranges all our habits around and in relationship to our spine.

Comfortable habits, behaviors and expressions favored by the conscious Self, are placed closer to the spine and higher up towards neck and head.

Uncomfortable habits, behaviors and expressions disfavored by Conscious Self, are located further away from the spine and lower down, "out of sight, is out of mind." Quite a few of these are relegated to our feet, our "misunderstandings" with Self, Others, World, God.

Q: What else has been uncovered about how we store habits-behaviors favored by Conscious Self?

A: Frequently accessed workable traits, memories, habits, behaviors and expressions, are located advantageously for quick access, relative to our spine:

- In front of us,

- At eye level,

- Closer in towards our spine

- On our right side, both inside and outside our skin envelope.

- Higher towards our heart and head, in and outside our skin.

Traits, memories, habits and behaviors NOT favored by our conscious self are placed in the 'storage room space' in our habit hologram:

- Behind us.

- On our LEFT side, inside and outside our skin.

- Outside our skin envelope.

The further outside our skin, the further away from our physical body, the more disowned this habit is by the conscious self.

Playing with a deck of Bridge cards is this action in human affairs. We hold close all the cards we believe are useful to us or soon may be useful. We discard cards we dislike and believe we have no use for. We literally dis-card intelligences and capabilities we believe are not valuable to us in the current game or current hand.

The pattern of how and where individuals disown and discard habits deemed not useful, is easier to see if we stand on a floor with a clock face on it. 12 Noon is straight ahead, six o'clock is behind us.

In the clock-face scheme, most of our psychological discards are sent to the locations represented between 6 and 9 o'clock.

This is true both horizontally and vertically. Disowned habits-memories-behaviors will be found in the left lower quadrant of a person's aura, as seen from behind, towards the left left leg and left foot; as well, as outside the skin in this same area.

A pattern of physical healing

Herring's Law in Homeopathy also applies. In general, humans tend to heal from the right side towards the left and from the head towards our feet.

Whatever our habit librarian determines is waste and residue is sent down towards our feet and/or to outside our body and under our feet. Clairvoyance is one way to perceive these things. If you're not clairvoyant, you can still self-test your way to perceive these areas. Making little diagrams on paper helped me to navigate.

The above suggests an updated experimental model for the psychological shadow: The shadow is primarily disowned habits, those Conscious Self prefers to keep outside of conscious awareness, on the outskirts of our psyche, by both intent and design. The majority of discarded learned habits-behavior patterns will be found outside our skin, behind us and to the left, approximately in the clock-face-quadrant between 6 and 9.

Shadow as blind spots in our psyche

Driver ed booklets show car drivers have two natural "blind spots." One is on our right between 4 and 5 o'clock. the other is on our left side between 7 and 8 o'clock.

Author's personal experience with his own shadow

I began exploring my shadow at the tender age of eight or nine thru the magazine, Famous Monsters of Filmland. I was fascinated with everything fantastic including monsters. My monsters were the "kinder gentler" kinds portrayed by Boris Karloff and animated by Ray Harryhausen.

This was early 1960s, before horror porn, before slasher porn, before sci-fi horror porn. Frankenstein, Dracula and the Wolfman were monsters you could almost bring home to mother. If you wish to re-capture the lovely innocence of the early monsters, look no further than Abbot and Costello Meet Frankenstein. Then Bride of Frankenstein.

I also had a 20 minute 8 mm version of the Bride of Frankenstein I projected on my wall with my friends over and over.

I dedicated myself to seeing all the monster movies I could access. In addition to traveling long distances by bike and bus to see Saturday afternoon movies, as a tween, I went to bed early Sat nite, setting my alarm to wake up at 11:00 PM to watch the late-night monster movies on TV. I did this every Saturday night for years.

To keep track of which films I had and had not seen, I kept a hand-written written list of all the monster movies I had seen. It was about 250 when I gave it up.

This was WAY before Jaws and Ridley Scott's Alien movie, when monsters were appropriated by corporate-commercial interests to see how much money they could make.

My mother became concerned with my interest in all things ugly and monstrous. She asked her hypnotist-counselor friend, Bea Clegg. Bea said, "Bruce regards monsters as beautiful." Looking back, I consider this insight compassionate. Bea captured my willingness to accept, identify and have compassion for classic monsters. She intuited I was looking for lost parts of myself. This was certainly true.

My interest in monsters and sci-fi led me naturally into hidden aspects of the sub- and unconscious and into metaphysics. Over decades this took me to Gestalt Two Chairs, Voice Dialogue, dowsing and self-muscle-testing as workable methods for my Hero's Journey.

From an online review of one of Debbie's books:

"One way to spot the dark side...is to pay attention to our over-reactions. If you find yourself getting all worked up when someone accuses you of being something you KNOW you are not, Ford tells us this reaction means you're right on top of some important information."

Both Bertrand Babinet and Debbie Ford point to excess reactivity as the first block and obstacle to personal-spiritual growing.

Any effort to consciously re-direct excessive reacting has the beneficial side-effect of increasing healthy self-discipline.

Q: What's the purpose or endgame of shadow work, working on your bad habits?

A: Debbie Ford is quoted in another online book review, "The purpose of doing shadow work, is to become whole. To end our suffering. To stop hiding ourselves from ourselves. Once we do this we can stop hiding ourselves from the rest of the world."

In my words, there is no better, easier place to work on our bad habits than here in the Earth experience. It's more difficult to work on them in every higher realm of existence. Since learned habits drive 95% of our behavior in the human experience, we have ample opportunity to focus on which habits are active, on each level, PACME. This is why some people, Like John-Roger, call the physical level "a springboard" for growth.

How much you attend to your habits, how much you get involved in realigning your habits with healthy upward spirals, is entirely up to you.

Why shadow work threatens people

Shadow work feels threatening to our small "s" self, ego, the one who knows when we take our last breath in the physical body, it's over for certain expressions.

Still, for those looking for transformational tools, shadow work is one of very few very direct paths.

Upgrading our self-concept requires going beyond and outside the box of our existing self-concept. Not everyone feels good enuf about themself to risk changing their self-concept.

It's often Life who challenges us to re-examine our self-concept. Shadow work is reinventing our self-concept, who we think we are, who we say we are and how we act in accord with who we think we are.

As we choose to re-align with upward spirals, life is a joyful journey more and more often.

Connection between Habit Body and self-concept

We identify mightily with the habits working for us today. That's natural.

Self-concept is again, nothing more than a bunch of habits: who and what we identify with the "good" parts of us (all workable, learned behaviors PACME, including role models we believe positive for us).

Our habits pertaining to self-concept are primarily sub- and unconscious. Identification with these habits intensifies them. Not a problem—until you want to change one of these. Or life tells you, those things you used to enjoy, those routines you were used to, they're no longer applicable, no longer workable. Change is coming.

When computers replace office workers, robots replace factory workers, the consequence technology boosters wish to downplay, ignore and dismiss is to the displaced workers. When workers are no longer needed for what they were trained to do, many displaced workers feel alienated. Their job and craft gave meaning, purpose and direction to their life. Take this away--your job is now self-re-invention, re-inventing your own purpose and direction. Not so easy if you lack language and methods to do so. Conceiving of a Habit Body facilitates language for self-reinvention.

Relating positively with our own shadow

Acting as Nurturing Parent to our Habit Body is a Best Practice in self-healing, for all inner child work, for Gestalt and Voice Dialogue work.

Acting as Nurturing Parent to our Habit Body means:

- acknowledging, then

- addressing, then

- locating a specific disturbance as best we can, then

- use whatever you have in your Healing Toolbox, and

- negotiate a new choice-habit-belief-behavior; and

- if you get stuck, seek people for support who have gone thru what you are going thru.

Q: Any worthwhile shadow literature today?

A: Debbie Ford's *Dark Side of the Light Chasers*. Beyond that, most literature on the psychological shadow is academic and technical in the extreme, unreadable to many Intuitive Feelers, the persons most likely to be interested and good at client support shadow work.

Rational science dismisses healthy shadow work

Q: Why is most literature on the shadow in our psyche excessively academic and technical?

A: This is partly historical. Psychology as a science, is very young, perhaps not even out of the diapers stage. Men hate admitting how little they know. Excessive academic and technical language makes men feel better, compensates for feeling inadequate about how little they know, about waking awareness.

Consider a group of blind men. None of them have ever seen an elephant, nor any picture of an elephant. They are now in the same room as a live elephant, trying to understand it without any sight. With his two hands, each touches only one part of the elephant. At first each blindman believes his one small part of the elephant, the leg, the tail, the trunk, to be the true character of the entire elephant.

Guess what? College-educated males, in the period 1800-1950 got ahold of the rational, left-brain intelligence in our psyche. They proclaimed, "Eureka! We found it! This one part is the whole of the Elephant of Consciousness!" Look no further! All other intelligences are illusory and must be dismissed!" This is how science became so one-sided, lop-sided and prone to endless creation of Frankenstein technologies.

While conscious awareness has more subjective validity and reality than any other Earthly experience--only the rational Thinking part of awareness was deemed "real" by the male blind men groping the Elephant of consciousness in the 1800s.

All other aspects of the Elephant were judged unreal, and dismissed. Without acknowledging the reality and validity of shadow work, no possibility exists to stop the endless reproducing of Dr. Frankenstein's monstrous technologies.

The religion of corporate-consumerism, a sub-set of one-sided science, is also prohibited from acknowledging let alone grappling with healthy Shadow work.

Anyone who tries to write about shadow literature quickly learns the mainstream lacks established rhetoric to work with. It's hard to write about.

There is also no 'one size fits all' solution. Shadow work is only real in the domain of one person at a time, very individual. There is no shadow work 'recipe' workable for everyone. Thinking for yourself, assembling your own methods, your own personal Healing Toolbox, is what works.

To Learn More

Find full discussion: *Goethean Holistic Science and the Three Sciences We Use Everyday for Holistic Practitioners and Self-Healers: Chapters 19-20 from Balance on All Levels-PACME+Soul Plus Related Essays*.

Chapter 11

Modern fairy tales about habits

Native American shadow story

A famous Native American story: One night an Indian chief talks to his son. "Two two dogs are inside my mind. One a white dog who is good and courageous, the other a black dog who is vengeful and spiteful. These two dogs are fighting to the death."

Concerned, the son asks, "Which one will win?"

The chief responds "The one I feed."

This images how our choices have consequences according to our innermost values.

The watch shop metaphor

Come with me and let's enter a typical European watch-clock shop of the 1800s. You see scores of watches and clocks displayed, on all four walls, some hanging from the ceiling, each one ticking away, doing what it knows how to do, as best it can, all of them displaying a time conforming with the local time zone.

There's no digital anything, no electricity. Vitality for each clock and watch is in the coiled spring, tiny or large each clock has.   `

It's an image of awesome intricacy for sure.

An individual watch and the watch shop as a whole, with dozens or hundreds of ticking watches, was commonly used as a metaphor for:

- the human psyche,

- for Nature on Earth,

- for the astronomical Universe as a whole.

The Clockwork Universe

In the history of science, the clockwork universe compares the universe to a mechanical clock. It continues ticking along, as a perfect machine, with its gears governed by the laws of physics, making every aspect of the machine predictable ~ Wikipedia In the 1800s, a popular metaphor was a 19th century European watch shop.

Each single habit we have indeed has much in common with a single watch, wound up by its owner, playing back one specific set function; until, it is wound up again.

Our Habit Body as a whole indeed has similarities to shop of hundreds of ticking watches, each performing its little routine function, each in its own pre-determined mechanism. In the Habit Body watch shop, ideally, all watches are synchronized to chime the same time of day in concert.

Watch shop as multiple logical systems in harmony

The clock shop image also captures the idea of multiple logical systems, multiple intelligences, all working in parallel, all aligned with a common function and aim; in this case, accurate local time.

What do we do in such a clock shop after admiring the handiwork?

We await the coming of the clockmaker, the watch maker. A living shop keeper must appear from time to time. He or she plays a pivotal role.

95% of the watch shop is ticking clocks. 5% is the clockmaker. Without the clockmaker winding the clocks on some schedule, all the clocks wind down to nothing and/or display erroneous times.

Our watch-shop-keeper has to supervise, tweak and wind his clocks repeatedly, some on a daily basis, to keep them functioning.

A child in a clock store like this, for the first time, might imagine 'one person—one clock.' "I'm like a clock!"

In actuality one adult is the manager of many timepieces. Like the watch-shopkeeper, our job is to keep all the ticking clocks coordinated, functioning together.

The Clockwork Universe metaphor died a natural death in scientific circles in the very early 1900s, during the time Einstein was productive.

The Clockwork Universe persevered in popular, mainstream imagination until the 1960s. The watch-clock shop metaphor for our functioning habits was finally replaced in the 1980s by a hologram metaphor for our psyche, thanks to Michael Talbot, in his Holographic Universe (1984, 2013).

Habit Body as hologram

"Hologram" was invented in the 1930s. It did not become part of mainstream culture until the 1970s when more and better color photographs became possible in magazines. A hologram and the adjective, "holographic," sum up much of what is observable in our Habit Body.

A hologram is a simpler—yet more etherealized—metaphor for our Habit Body than a watch shop. Take your pick. Which is more workable for you now?

After muscle testing and self-testing arrived, the idea of our habits in a fractal hologram formation became so big, it became a booklet, *You Are a Hologram Becoming Visible to Yourself* (2012).

One big reason all academic-mainstream-corporate psychology of the 1900s now seems so out of date and dating more each day, is it is built on the fragile paradigm of the line, linear sequences, cause and effect and mostly only in one direction.

Since Holographic Universe (1984) it's been easy to shift to a 3D model of our psyche based on the metaphor of a hologram.

A hologram is not linear-sequential, not based on the line. It's based on the whole, in multiple dimensions, is always greater than the sum of its individual parts.

Most of 20th century mainstream psychology--and ALL of 19th century psychology, was hoping to understand our psyche as a mental system. Now we know more and have more sophisticated and accurate models.

The mental level of PACME is literally too low a level, too granular, to understand our psyche as a whole. Imagine trying to understand a clock with another clock. Not much happens; the function of one merely reflects the other.

To understand a Habit Body storing habits of feeling-thinking, you have to go above thinking-feeling to the etheric level, where all the templates are. That's where the real learning is, the Unconscious patterns behind what we have on a lower level as everyday thinking-feeling.

Our rational-mental function is a useful, sub-function of the whole hologram of our psyche. Our psyche is NOT primarily a mental system; it's not a jigsaw puzzle, not a clockwork. It is more "organic" yet still employs Sacred Geometry, at a higher level, just above the mind, in our etheric body.

Habit Body as Rubik's Cube

A Rubik's Cube gives our mind a way of thinking about how change occurs in our habit hologram: one face, one facet, becomes more coherent, integrated and aligned; while at the same time, another of the six faces is thrown out of alignment.

This is commonly observable in healthy change work with clients: one complaint subsides, quiets down, recedes into the background. The next most disturbed internal part comes to forward; it becomes foreground in our psyche.

How do we "solve" an organic Rubik's Cube? Generally we keep turning it to learn where it is most out of balance, address the most distressed face of the cube, then the next distressed and so on. This is precisely how our immune system works.

Unworkable habits as "my issues"

What is an issue anyway? Again, simply another basket of habits. More helpfully, my issues are any choice, habit, behavior or memory I identify as not longer workable for me now.

What's usually happening is our comfort zone, our Habit Body, is in conflict with our consciously held values.

Take X. X can be money, food, sex, social status, victimhood--anything. If we identify with X, and X is defined as part of our comfort zone; then, the basic self will hold onto and try to preserve X, no matter how painful it is to hold onto and sustain X.

When I begin to dis-identify with X and say, "That's not me anymore," then re-directing the energy of old habit X becomes possible.

My Habit Body will only release X when it's convinced this is the intention of Conscious Waking Self. Just saying to yourself, "I really should stop smoking" rarely convinces a person's Habit Body they mean business.

Q: Yes but I know a guy who said, "I'm stopping smoking today" and that was the last time he ever smoked.

A: I meet these people occasionally too. Guess what? They already have healthy, effective two-way communication between Conscious Self and Habit Body. Enuf positive self-esteem building activities are on-going, Habit Body can easily drop one habit and not feel any big loss.

Q: But I thought Conscious Self is also the stand-in representative for our immortal-eternal soul?

A: You got it. When the two lower selves of the Three Selves, Conscious Self and Habit Body are connecting, communicating and looking forward to tomorrow, if C/s says to let go of habit X, Habit Body listens. It acknowledges the authority of soul shines thru C/s. This is how intention can be powerful in personal change work. Don't leave home without it.

Chapter 12

Redirecting habits in children and adults

The other day someone said, "The perfect parent is someone with a cogent child-rearing method-philosophy–and no children."

The Plan for human beings was taking loving care of infants and young children as a reminder to accept and cooperate with our own basic self.

Q: Where can I learn healthy approaches to infant and childcare?

A: For re-directing habits in children, please see:

- *Birth Without Violence* book and film,

- Resources for Infant Educators (RIE),

- La Leche League,

- Waldorf-methods education

Rahima Baldwin's book, *You Are Your Child's First Teacher* (2nd edition preferred) has the most to say gathered in one place on healthy parenting and mentoring of children. Find this book easily at libraries. *Teaching As A Lively Art*, by Marjorie Spock (baby and child care Benjamin Spock's sister) is a gem also. It overviews holistic child-development clearly and with humor.

- Rudolf Dreikurs in *Positive Discipline* by Jane Nelson.

For re-directing adult habits-behavior I suggest:

- Compassionate (nonviolent) Communication (NVC). 30-40 hours of videos on YouTube.

For counselors: Thomas Gordon's Parent Effectiveness Training (PET) (www.gordontraining.com). Gordon's take on active listening and cooperation is more about mentoring.

For teens and adults of all ages, a wow is Choice Theory; a new psychology of personal freedom, William Glasser. A comprehensive and practical philosophy based around the wisdom, magic and sacredness of choice.

For adults, redirecting habits means re-training yourself. What does this mean? Self-discipline. Adults retrain themselves experimentally one baby-step experiment at a time.

Not everyone is ready for this, for committing to committing to your self, committing to deliberate and conscious negotiation with your own Child Within. If you are, let's go.

Changing habits thru willpower

The most common model we have for changing-upgrading habits is from extraverted sports: change your outer performance at tennis, football, weightlifting, etc thru willpower, practice, practice, practice to achieve better physical results.

That's fine. I did this as a child and as a runner and at the gym.

Problem is the Sports Willpower Method often is missing the Inner Game os Sports half, laid out by Tim Gallway first in the Inner Game of Tennis (1971), building on the 1948 Herigel classic, Zen and the Art of Archery.

Since the 1970s, the modern sports model to improve performance is to attend to BOTH the Inner Game of your sport as well as the Outer Game of your sport, two Games, not one, an introverted Game and an extraverted Game.

The best sports improvement theory for kids is always going to be largely practice, commitment and dedication. Modern sports performance enhancement for adults is always going be a COMBINATION of attending to both Games in your sport.

Extraverted sports performance improvement training is always going to a wonderful preparation, a wonderful metaphor, for the more subtle inner reordering of behavior required to move sub- and unconscious habits.

The outer Sports model of habit change meets its downfall when applied to codependency and other unconscious addictions.

If the behavior you wish to redirect is more hidden, outside and below the perception of your thinking mind, revving up your willpower and using it like a hammer or bulldozer is unlikely to work.

The deeper, the more unconscious the behaviors you wish to move are, the less well the hammer of willpower, YANG, right-sided energy, will be effective.

What works? Attending to the Two Games of any habit you wish to change, upgrade or re-direct. You must re-parent yourself. Conscious Self re-parents the Habit Body like a child, assisting it to get its needs met in better, healthier ways.

We were all more lovable when we were young

Why do we love little babies and baby animals so much? Newborn animals and humans are like open windows, openings thru which unconditioned energy can flow thru to us. Spirit flows thru like water thru a hole in a concrete dam.

We are at our most lovable as unconditioned infants, before our later habits form and stop unconditioned flow.

Then what happens? As babies mature, conditioning starts being absorbed and accumulates. Habits arrive thru conditioning.

"Care-voyance"

Because the inner child is invisible, the truth of it must be perceived inwardly, personally, and individually. You do not have to be clairvoyant to perceive your Three Selves. You do have to listen and watch with loving sensitivity. A world-famous Waldorf teacher, Eugene Schwartz calls this "care-voyance."

Redirecting habits in animals, training a new puppy

This section applies to all pets. The dynamics are most visible with dogs. Dogs, in the hands of their owners, go thru similar training to what our Habit Body goes thru at the "hands" of adults and the conscious self. Dogs must be shown

- not to make messes,

- what food to eat, what food not to eat,

- not to injure self or others,

- to cooperate with schedules,

- to control excessive anger and joy that inflicts on others.

- to accept reasonable restraints for safety reasons (leash),

- that they cannot have everything they want whenever they want it (self-control)

Some dog owners are very effective in dog training. Then—there is the rest of us.

Dog training challenges can be due to:

- ignoring the authentic needs of the pet

- overestimating the pet's intelligence (unwillingness to go down to the pet's level of understanding and negotiate there)

- projecting the owner's lack of foresight and errors in judgment onto the pet.

When a dog-owner relationship is healthy, what happens?

- The owner admires her pet's positive qualities and strengths.

- A mutual respect for needs occurs.

- Love and affection is exchanged.

If you wish a new behavior in your puppy, you have to repeat the new behavior–consciously–enuf times for the basic self to pick it up and adopt the new behavior. You want the puppy to imitate you, to follow your lead.

Waldorf educators call "learning thru repetition" imitative thinking. Habits learned thru repetition are nothing to sneeze at. I estimate over 50% of our learning, conception to age nine, appears to be learning thru repetition. Where would we be without breathing, walking, stopping at red lights, reading, writing, saying goodbye and so on. We have thousands of behaviors learned thru repetition.

Not kill, not "get rid of:" redirect, re-educate, heal, redeem

B.F. Skinner liked to talk of "extinguishing undesirable behaviors." Whenever our Habit Body hears this kind of language, it resists. It knows:

- search-and-destroy

- eliminating

- doing away with, and

- eradicating

...are words of againstness and non-cooperation.

Skinner was magical with his pigeons, training them for example to walk in a figure eight, by feeding it food from his hand, simply by how he reinforced it.

Despite his "magic" with animals, he never seemed to connect with his own inner child; and, was dramatically and famously a failure with the behavior mod experiments he performed on his own daughter.

You can't do away with any part of your own psychic energy. Telling the basic self you are going to eliminate a habit is like telling the basic self you are going to cut off a hand. The basic self is primarily habits! It's job is to maintain habits on all levels PACME. Our inner child does the best job it can do to maintain each and every habit that the c/s has set in motion.

The c/s is god to the basic self. To say "I'm going to "extinguish this habit" tells the basic self, "I am going to kill part of you." How cooperative do you think the average basic self is going to be with this approach to altering habits?

You can't do away with any part of your own psychic energy. You can repress it; you can suppress it; you can project it. You can send it off to Siberia in your consciousness, where it will sit in the outskirts of your aura, to be projected on the next likely screen coming down the road. Better is to redirect, reform, transform and mature up these energies. Give them new healthy jobs. But you cannot get rid of your own unresolved energies. That's just repression.

Since at least John Bradshaw's time, we talk about redirecting, altering, upgrading and maturing up habits. Habits are energy. Like clay they can be re-shaped and. NLP in the 1980s was very healthy on this point also, emphasizing the "ecological check" when doing change work.

You can redirect, reform, transform, redeem and mature-up your energies. Give them new jobs, healthier habits. Habits are no more or less than conditioned behavior. You move out the old prior conditioning and move in the new positive conditioning. You recalibrate your energy there to the energy of loving in your own heart.

Metaphor of the Good Shepherd

The best metaphor I've found so far for redirecting wayward habits and behaviors is the "Good Shepherd."

HOW does the Good Shepherd redeem his "lost sheep"? By learning at what stage his wayward sheep is on this sequence, then dialoging with it to move it to the next stage.

Acknowledgement > Acceptance > understanding >

compassion > forgiveness >

negotiating new behavior > resolution

The Good Shepherd goes after each and every lost sheep and redeems it back into the fold, back into the community of sheep gathered around the warm circle of the Shepherd's campfire. That's a healthy picture of the mature and loving c/s. In healthy growth, we upgrade habits. Spiritual growth is upgrading our habits on any level.

"The poem of the Good Shepherd"

The good shepherd loves all his sheep.

He hears the bleating of his lost sheep.

It's only the gray and black ones who are lost,

My bad habits and behaviors.

Does the good shepherd ignore the cries for help?

The good shepherd, the conscious self, goes to assist.

The shepherd leaves the Light and warmth

Of his comfortable campfire in the wilderness.

He goes out into the darkness

To find his sheep.

With all his being

He listens and looks

In every direction in the dark.

Oh, there it is

Hung up on some barbed wire,

Can't get free by itself.

The good shepherd extricates his charge

With firm, tender care.

He assists, not helps

The lamb to free itself

From where it was caught in the world.

The good shepherd lifts up his sheep

Leads it back into the Light.

The lamb rejoins the flock

Around the Light and warmth of the shepherd's campfire.

Whenever a lamb is redeemed

The shepherd is happy.

He's done his job. Peace expands.

Then he hears the next sheep

Out there, bleating in it's darkness.

Are you a Good Shepherd

to your own wayward habits?

In healthy growth, when we change a habit, we upgrade the habit. Spiritual growth is upgrading our habits on any level.

Further discussion of Behaviorism can be found in any psyche intro text. I recommend Gerald Corey's Theory and Practice of Counseling and Psychotherapy.

If the basic self has to learn its lessons all alone

Charles Whitfield's book, *Healing the Child Within* (Health Communications 1987), was a major distributor of the idea of the inner child in the 1980s. Whitfield reprints a poem by Portia Nelson, "Autobiography in five short chapters." It details default learning, how we all learn if the inner child has received no training in how to cooperate with the c/s and must do everything unassisted.

"Autobiography in five short chapters"

1) I walk down the street.

There is a deep hole in the sidewalk.

I fall in.

I am lost. I am hopeless.

It isn't my fault.

It takes forever to find a way out.

2) I walk down the same street.

There is a deep hole in the sidewalk.

I pretend I don't see it.

I fall in again.

I can't believe I'm in the same place.

But it isn't my fault.

It still takes a long time to get out.

3) I walk down the same street.

There is a deep hole in the sidewalk.

I see it is there.

I still fall in--it's a habit.

My eyes are open.

I know where I am.

It IS my fault.

I get out immediately.

4) I walk down the same street.

There is a deep hole in the sidewalk.

I walk around it.

5) I walk down another street.

(c) Portia Nelson 1980, from the book of poems, *There's a Hole in My Sidewalk: The Romance of*

Self-Discovery. Beyond Words Publishing Company, 1994. ISBN: 0941831876. Popular Library edition, 1980. (reprint permission requested but the owner of the poem did not respond so far).

Portia's poem describes how basic selves learn, if left entirely to themselves. It's not pretty; it's not efficient; it does work. Our rate of learning increases rapidly when the conscious self takes active, loving interest. Is there any area where this is not true? The most effective interventions are always love and self-forgiveness.

Growth is upgrading our habits on any level

Our preferred ways of reacting to life run on automatic unless and until we make conscious choices to isolate one of those habit patterns and take the time to upgrade and redirect a habit.

That's "learning." That's "positive change," the refrain of this booklet.

Awareness of and direction of our own habit patterns, especially when done in microscopic baby steps—consistently—over time--is perhaps THE most powerful tool for personal-spiritual growing.

Our conscious thinking self is uniquely suited to identifying dysfunctional habit patterns and instituting correction, improvement and upgrade.

We can all afford to slow down and gain an improved alphabet of concepts about habits, according to the Three Selves.

More Broadly, Culture, personality and destiny are all largely a function of habits.

Conventional wisdom tells us this in the familiar aphorism from Heraclitus, "Character is destiny."

In a manner of speaking, our Habit Body is our destiny—unless and until we redirect it. This is more precise.

Chapter 13

Habit Body as "Reactivity"

Reactivity is our best friend

A sad conventional wisdom is often heard, "If people knew better, they would DO better." More precisely we can now say, 'If a person's Habit Body knew how to do better, the person would do better.'

What's sad to me is not that "people do not do better;" rather, how little intention, time and effort individuals put into exploring their own Habit Body; and then, upgrading outworn and obsolete memories, habits, behaviors and expressions they find there.

I'm going to say something next which may only become clear at the book's end. Saying it here because it is the key people are looking for—once you have eyes to see it.

Maturing-up (wisdom) includes making more and quicker distinctions between who "I" am in my 5%; and on the other hand, the canned, rehearsed expressions I play back to other people and the world thru my Habit Body.

Perhaps this will be clearer: Maturing-up (wisdom) includes making more and better distinctions between myself as a capital "S" self, me as soul, on one hand and, who "I" am here, only temporarily, in the 3D world, my small "s" self, my habits, my behaviors. Both are worthy of love, education and up-leveling.

Forgiveness remains one of the most fun, practical ways to love our self and our Self. I as a soul, my immortal-eternal Self needs forgiveness. So do my behaviors, actions and habits: "To err is human." Find the full Forgiveness exercise in *Forgive from Your Soul, Slow-Motion Forgiveness: The Missing Manual, Forgiveness 101 How-to Book* (New Directions In Brain Balance) (Volume 4)

WHY WE Deal with reactivity first

Most of our roadblocks and detours in personal-spiritual growing are characterized as excess reactivity. Reactivity is what pulls us out of balance pretty much first, last and always.

Reactivity can work for or against our health, wealth and happiness. It is good when we snatch an opening for a kiss from our sweetie. When we like to eat jelly doughnuts every day or dislike our mother-in-law before we ever meet her—and can't stop ourselves—then reactivity is pulling us out of balance.

Excess reactiveness is what pulls us way from doing the things we know work for us to produce health, wealth and happiness.

Most of the time we are reacting too quickly to life (John-Roger). To change or reduce your own reactivity—first it helps to appreciate what it does for you and understand it.

We need reactivity to cross a busy street and not get hit by a car. If we did not react, if were crossing a street on foot and saw a car bearing down on us, without reactions, we would have to think, "Now what, if anything does this have to do with me?"

Or if our wife smiles and touches our arm in a soft and gentle caress, without reactions we would only be able to think, "Now why is she doing this?" With reactions we move first, think later.

Reactivity has many good uses! It's the major sense organ the soul has here in 3D. If we are smart, we give our reactivity its due and use it to our advantage.

To Learn More: Reactivity Is Our Best Friend, New Directions in Holistic Brain Balance (Vol 3).

How much excess reactivity do I have?

You know you have a lot of reactivity if you find yourself saying this a lot:

"I knew it was bad for me and I did it anyway."

"I knew I shouldn't have eaten it but I ate it anyway."

"I knew I shouldn't have said that but I said it anyway."

"I knew it was bad for me but I went and did it anyway."

Many times we are simply reacting to life and reacting too quickly. Reactivity affects us like this: Our inner child is in part our capacity to react and to respond subconsciously and unconsciously. This is our Habit Body. The inner child is--among other things--our Habit Body.

Occasionally, Conscious Self allows Inner Child to react with outbursts of emotion. Mostly, Inner Child is reacting unconsciously, not monitored by Conscious Self. Inner Child is the seat, the home, of our reactivity, healthy and unhealthy. While we are here on Earth, we are constantly faced with the habits it's learned and whether to allow them or stop and improve a habit.

The Earth experience seems to be designed for us to clear karma. Much of our karma is habits we have set in motion in the past now in need of upgrading and realignment.

Q: Upgraded and realigned with what?

A: With your own deepest, innermost values, whatever you got. 'Soul is choice' so your alignment is up to you. You are what you align with. You can align any way you like. Sooner or later you'll learn how workable your alignment is.

The mechanism of dilemma and stuckness

An individual who "enjoys smoking" cigarettes can resist a lot of peer pressure to stop smoking. Perceiving we "have too much to lose" operates even more strongly among groups of people. The dilemma about giving up unhealthy choices can be seen on a macro level in the dilemma about war and militarism.

Militarism, using force against force in the present world situation, rarely works well. Yet the collective military-industrial-congressional complex does not feel able to give up using force against force.

Militarism is stimulating on so many levels, to give it up for peace and diplomacy, for few jobs making bombs and planes to fly them, a lowered level of sensory stimulation, seems like too much of a sacrifice.

For peace to become attractive to an individual, peace has to be high on their scale of values. With this in place, then, healthy leadership can coordinate group movement towards greater benefits for the majority.

A surplus of self-esteem has to be present in order to risk new behavior. Choosing change requires emotional capital to make change. A mood of expansion is the pre-requisite to try new things.

The basic self has to feel supported from outside or inside, be in a mood of expansion towards proposed change. Without feeling expansive, it's likely to hold on to what it had yesterday.

Where is reactivity in my body?

We have reactivity in both our gut brain and head brain. In our gut brain, reactivity is primarily located in the sub-conscious and unconscious halves of the solar plexus.

Reactivity anatomy #1 top & bottom

SUBconscious

-----------o-----------

UNconscious

The little circle marks your belly button. For simplicity's sake, we are ignoring quadrants

Reactivity anatomy #2 with quadrants

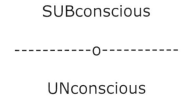

The

Identifying and locating reactivity is taken up much more thoroly in The Inner Court.

A quadrant model is useful for locating where a disturbance is relative to the body. For a fuller discussion of this

Reactivity is primarily in the sub-conscious and unconscious levels of the solar plexus (Bertrand Babinet):

Liking and disliking occurs in the subconscious above the belly button, with the quality we call "feeling."

Liking and disliking occur equally in the UNconscious below our belly button, with the quality we call "willingness."

This model is useful for locating where a disturbance is relative to the front of the human body. Full Discussion in the Holistic Brain Balance booklet series.

Liking in behavioral terms

Liking-sympathy for something, in moderation, like food, is good—too much liking and sympathy becomes a problem over time.

Liking-sympathy for specific people, places, things reinforces them as part of our identified comfort zone.

Disliking-antipathy against specific people, places, things can be good, such as saying "no" to high commercial bank charges by switching all your money and accounts to a credit union. Too much disliking and antipathy against the IRS or the government can get you put in jail.

We use disliking-antipathy to set up boundaries between us and our comfort zones and everything we identify as outside our comfort zones.

Reactivity can be looked at as excess sympathies and antipathies, excess liking and disliking.

"Reducing excess sympathies and antipathies"

I've found Rudolf Steiner's phrase, "reducing our excess sympathies and antipathies" (1919) very useful. Reducing our excess sympathies and antipathies is a pretty good definition of maturation, of personal growth.

Any excess over- or under-reacting I remove from my Habit Body Reduce clears my path of growth, fewer behaviors distracting me from choosing what is workable for me. Maturation is in part outgrowing our excess sympathies and antipathies, a healthy process.

When I avoid, delay and deny the presence of my excess reactivity, I delay my further maturity. The more spoiled I am, the weaker my self-discipline muscles are, the more I am living according to my pre-programmed Habit Body running on automatic, sub- and unconsciously.

Excess liking-sympathy defined

Liking-sympathy is the "bring it to me" half of reactivity.

Excess sympathy is an unexamined pull towards choosing any person, place or belief, you consciously know is unhealthy for you.

With excess sympathy, we react to things favorably--even when they are bad for us. We like chocolate cake, even when we are on a low carb diet. The battered wife returns to the abusive husband because he is all she knows.

Excess disliking-antipathy defined

Antipathy-disliking is the pushing away, "take it away," half of reactivity.

With excess disliking, we react to things unfavorably, even when it's healthy for us. The two year old says, "I hate spinach." The twenty year old says, "I hate putting money in my savings account." The fifty year old says, "I hate exercise."

Excess DISliking is similar to under-participation. Pick a target you wish to evaluate. On a scale of 100, if optimal participation is 50/100, not too much, not too little—how's your participation in the target?

How excess antipathy becomes "gossip"

If somebody we consider an enemy does something laudable, good, and honest, excess antipathy can prompt us to say, "Yes, but they had ulterior motives." Excess antipathy towards an individual can prevent us from seeing a person as ever doing good.

Without addressing my own excess reactivity further, maturity may elude me. It's possible now for those wishing to, to address excess reactivity systematically. The tools are here. It's a journey of self-examination leading to self-discipline, improved self-esteem and improved self-concept.

Feeling sympathy~antipathy for the same person

Difficulty arises when we feel sympathy~antipathy for the same person. Did you ever feel conflicted towards your Mom or your Dad, for instance? This is why in Gestalt Therapy, Fritz Perls taught people to acknowledge both their resentments and their appreciations, their antipathies and their sympathies towards the same person.

It's possible to have both excess-liking, excess-disliking towards the same thing at the same time. This dynamic may be uncovered in a clinical situation; such as, a battered wife uncovering she feels both exaggerated liking and exaggerated disliking for her spouse.

The technical metaphysical term for both "excess liking-sympathy" and "excess disliking-antipathy" is "excess astrality."

Q: Which is worse, excess sympathy or excess antipathy?

A: Like a plucked rubber band, reactivity vibrates on either side of center, both right and left equally. Our most complex difficulties occur with a combination of excess sympathy and excess antipathy.

The conventional solution? Healthy detachment, healthy self-discipline; like, being the firm but loving Nurturing Parent of a cranky three year old.

Excess reactivity is almost always telling us we have an old habit in place worth examining more closely. What behavior would be more aligned with my core values?

We have a comfort zone on each level PACME. Working to purify our Habit Body of excess reactivity can feel like working with five different Habit Bodies. It can feel like a Heroes Journey to do this work. The good news? Anything we wish to change in ourselves, is no more nor less, than finding and re-directing the relevant habits. This paraphrases a big part of NLP's message.

The "Ewwwww!" reflex

A quick test exists of how much acceptance and tolerance the c/s has for the basic self level. Simply think about these:

- blood

- urine

- mucus

- feces

to cooperate with schedules,

Whorovor you have the "Ewwwww!!!" reaction, this measures the antipathy and fear habituated into conscious Self towards the lower, basic self.

Conversely the less reactive the c/s is towards blood and bodily products, the more accepting the c/s tends to be towards the basic self level. Acceptance is a prerequisite for cooperation.

The above insight seems to be the explanation for at least one radical form of physical healing. A radical approach to healing, that has worked for some people for almost one hundred years. The method? Drinking small amounts of your own urine for healing. The literature on this speculates beneficial effects come from ingesting the antibodies excreted in the urine. Drinking your urine recycles your own antibodies and gives you–

theoretically–more antibodies to fight off whatever disease you are working on.

Another dynamic here is perhaps more potent. Tasting your own urine is so fraught with cultural taboos and such a different taste experience, both the c/s and basic self are immediately thrust together and must ENGAGE. Many basic selves have such an extreme aversion to this, they will DO ANYTHING not to be forced to drink urine again. They will even get well! You can almost hear the basic self say, "Stop! Okay, okay, I'll get the body well! Just don't make me drink that stuff again!"

Hey, if it gets you well, then it worked for you.

Reactivity overcharged~undercharged

Excess liking and excess dis-liking connects with over-participation and under-participation (Babinetics).

Most of our 'reactivity language' attends to OVERcharged liking (infatuation, puppy love, lust, passion, etc)

and,

OVERcharged DISliking (anger, rudeness, spiteful, revengeful, hatred, blaming others, scapegoating, violence, prejudice etc).

However, guess what? UNDERcharged liking~disliking are just as worthy of attention.

UNDERcharged liking (failing to say "please" and "thank you," lack of good manners, lack of diplomacy, looking a gift horse in the mouth, not counting your blessings, under-appreciation of spouse, children, co-workers, etc.)

and,

UNDERcharged DISliking (complicity with evil,
"going along with the crowd" when you know it's
immoral and unethical, passive-aggressive, not
standing up for your rights and your own voice,
not speaking truth to power when possible,
permitted and clear for you to do, depression,
suicide).

Animals have an Instinct Body

Q: My psyche must contain thousands of habits.
How come I don't fall down in a confused fit?

A: Humans can accommodate many more habits
than instinct alone permits animals. How? Our
etheric body is more sophisticated and nuanced
than the etheric body of mammals-animals.

The human Habit Body is multi-dimensional far
beyond the few levels of function your pet dog or
cat has. An approximate comparison: Our Habit
Body spans across sleeping, dreaming and
waking. The etheric bodies of pets and animals
only encompass sleeping and dreaming.

In large part, our animal pets live primarily in
their Instinct Body. It plays back pre-
programmed responses to prompts received thru
their five animal senses, not much more. We still

find joy in this. Every intelligence level is worthy of love.

The human Habit Body is far more sophisticated, even compared to the higher apes. Our most wakeful, human work of making new, healthy decisions each day is primarily outside of the Habit Body, in the 5% where we have free choice.

Chapter 14

Why so difficult to change my habits?

Individuals can and do re-directing old habits into more workable behavioral patterns.

What's required? 90% of the time the direct, deliberate intervention of Conscious Waking Self is required.

The other 10% Your habits can be changed by accident, by moving to a new country, etc.

What makes us think it's difficult to change a habit is lack of adequate and sufficient education on the nature of our Habit Body and he Power Within Us which in the waking human experience is healthy choosing.

A rat in a man-made maze will come up against a dead end, sniff it out for an opening. If no opening, the rat avoids coming the same way again. If the rat finds a way out of the maze, it drops any other path it was following more or less immediately and takes only the path that gets it to food.

Habit Body 2nd ed ~ 197

Put an adult male in a maze. If he comes upon a dead end, he may look around for a few minutes. Then he will sit down--and sit there–or bang his head on the wall–or leave and return to the same stuck spot over and over–and maybe never go look for a new way around the obstacle. A human may even die at a dead end without ever exploring outside his own expectations and mental comfort zones

Why is this?

We can change our mind CONsciously, At the same time our SUBconscious mind and UNconscious mind can go blithely on doing today what they did yesterday and expect to do tomorrow.

The deliberate intervention of Conscious Waking Self is usually required to help these parts of us "get the memo" they did not get or did not read.

Our difficulty in changing a habit once established can also be the dilemma of, "I have too much to lose, I've invested too much, to change now." The human being has conditioning on all levels PACME. The rat does not. The human being has a hard time practicing trial and error in any pure way.

For the rat to abandon a blind alley with a dead end is easy. It has very few to no conditioning mentally-emotionally or in memories, pulling on it to follow a familiar path. It has only the physical to lose, so to speak. These other levels humans have, emotions, mind and memories, are strongly influential on human behavior. Each level of PACME, and in this order, is approximately a power of ten more potent that the realm of the letter to the left. They pull on us mightily.

To try something new, the human being has to give up choices made on all levels PACME.

Unless the person sees a realistic possibility of gaining some advantage by dropping old choices and experimenting with new ones, why should they give up all those choices it has made up to this point? After all, didn't they work up to this point?

Of course this is exactly what life asks us to do, to give up choices not working for us, and try something new, no matter how invested we are in old choices. That's why it's harder for us than for a rat. We have more to lose than a rat does.

Chapter 15

Why are addictions so addictive?

Thru repetition, habits build up strength and "momentum." Thru for both desirable and undesirable habits.

We're all here learning to become better managers of our habits.

We have learned-conditioned behaviors physically, imaginally, emotionally, mentally and mythologically (PACME).

In each of these frequencies, I have functional and DYSfunctional habits. So any "addiction" is a subset of all dysfunctional habits in my Habit Body.

How individuals access and leverage change here is highly individual. Custom work is almost always required; some of this you can do yourself. The only limit to how much self-healing you can do, is the depth of your self-connection.

The 95% to 5% split between habits and conscious-waking choosing, means soul in the human experience remains in a precarious position. 5% of our waking psyche is tasked with managing and balancing the other 95% of our psyche.

When the momentum and inertia of existing habits overwhelms soul in an individual, and undesirable habits are allowed to play and replay to others and the world; then, established DYSfunctional habits become "addictions."

The 5% of choice needs support to interrupt and redirect the force, momentum and inertia of well-established habit patterns.

Some addictive patterns

What kind of unhealthy habits and addictions do I most commonly see as a Health Intuitive? If you think drugs, alcohol, smoking and sex are at the top of the list, you are wrong.

Shopping

Guilt

Worry

Victimizing others or playing the victim

Blaming self or others

Self-criticism

Over-extending ourselves to others

Fixing and rescuing others

Television

Rigid fundamentalism, rigid beliefs, views

including: impractical, vaguely conceived

New Age abstractions like "soul-mate" & "Law of Attraction"

Slightly revised from Health Intuition (p. 40-41), Karen Grace Kassy, "Most common addictions I see as a Health Intuitive"

When beliefs are addictions

Bernie Siegel says, "People are addicted to their beliefs. If you try to change someone's deeply-held belief, they act like an addict." A religious fanatic might kill you if you try to take the drug of his religion away.

This also suggests why so many scientific advances require the old generation to die off first. Old habits, old beliefs, die hard. The

Establishment is only too willing to punish those who stray from established "comfortable" beliefs.

Remember the priests who refused to look through Galileo's telescope? New innovations and clearer language challenge us to re-examine long-held beliefs and language constructs. This is easier for younger minds and those who remain young at heart.

"Habits are the etheric body fallen into matter"

Dennis Klocek, of Rudolf Steiner College, said in a 2000 lecture, "Habits are the etheric body fallen into matter." This is a two-edged sword, both good news and bad news.

On the good side, if habits were not a fallen expression of our etheric body, how would you remember your name from one day to the next? It may also be true that "instincts" are " the etheric body fallen into matter" at least those not specifically determined by genes, if you can discern the difference between genes and habits and which came first, chicken or egg?

On the bad side, historically and in present day human experience, our etheric body easily becomes preoccupied with the mere minutiae of physical level survival and maintenance. Unless you live in a monastery or nunnery, little time to allow your e-body to expand to its full capacity and embrace a gentle upward spiral. In survival mode, our e-body gets hypnotized into a reality composed of primarily downward spirals.

Creation is all conditioned energy, PACME, the field of habits in this Creation. Habits are what hold things in place in Creation, closely related to inertia.

Soul and above is UN-conditioned energy, as in unconditional love. Habits do not exist here as they do outside in conditioned creation.

What holds things in place in soul and above is devotion, and alignment as moment to moment choices, free choices. Re-directing our own Habit Body is terrific training for this. All of us here in 3D are gods in training.

Chapter 16

Our habits around pain, PACME

Want to find the comfort zones of your Habit Body? You can easily find it in any behaviors around avoiding pain & discomfort.

Animals avoid physical pain and discomfort of any kind. Ever try to give a cat a bath or make them swallow a pill of medicine? Only conscious Self has intelligence to grasp taking a bath or swallowing a pill has greater value than the discomfort involved. Whenever you avoid pain and/or discomfort, the basic self is active.

The good news here is the basic self does its best to help us avoid pain and unnecessary experiences.

Physical pain is primarily experienced by our basic self, not by Conscious Self. This is why people, especially in the West today, can be walking around, even going to work, in moderate to quite severe physical pain. The gap between the basic self and Conscious/s is sufficient in adults so the c/s can still function even in the presence of severe physical pain. Conscious Self can make the basic self go to work even if the basic self is experiencing severe pain, as is the case with some persons with cancer or sprained ankles. Work habits can be strong as our self-esteem and self-concept are often based on them.

Physical pain in children before puberty

What happens when a child before age nine is in physical pain? Everything stops. The conscious self is out of commission until the boo-boo or worse is attended to. This makes perfect sense as before age nine, Conscious/s and basic self are still more converged than distinct. Later in life gut-brain~head-brain will permit more of a two-fold inner experience. Before age 9, more of a unified inner experience.

Q: What about moving money around to avoid the pain of taxes? Is the basic self active there?

A: This is not physical pain. Looking bad to the IRS is painful only to the conscious self. It's closer to social embarrassment and looking bad in comparison to your moral values. Other pain primarily felt by the c/s, includes looking bad in an intellectual community, plagiarizing from a book to finish your own. Lying to Congress would be another.

Pain PACME

You won't be surprised to hear pain exists on all levels PACME. Consider:

Guess who tracks all of these and maintains them until cleared up? You got it, the basic self.

We have habits on each
of five frequencies of our psyche

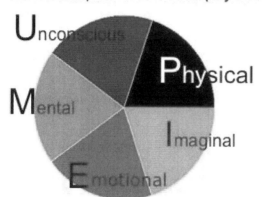

ne short
f records and
 3D
s many
nultitude of
rtunities to
iaviors which
can correct

Tony Robbins on constructive use of pain

In many of his recorded materials, Anthony Robbins is big on educating his audiences to the positive use of pain on all levels. He talks like this. Say you have an idea for a book: a coffee table book about coffee tables as Kramer did on Seinfeld. Tony says if this is your dream, then you can use pain positively two ways. First you can articulate to yourself the benefits of success with your invention: money, fame, women, new house, TV interviews, women, new car, women, etc. This is what you direct your Habit Body towards: bigger benefits and bigger comfort zones.

Second, you can articulate to yourself the pain you will experience if you gIve up on your great idea: feel like you'll never amount to anything, poverty, feel like a failure, etc.

In his seminars, books, tapes, DVDs Tony shows people how to associate pleasure with their positive goals; and, associate more pain with the consequences of not pursuing the goal. Emphasizing pain can also be used to redirect unwanted behavior like overeating, lack of commitment, etc. Tony amplifies this with NLP techniques to help students arrange things inside themselves so pleasure is associated with their goals and pain is associated with the behaviors they wish to put behind them.

This amounts to a carrot and stick strategy; send your Habit Body towards the positive and away from negative consequences. If done with rigor and precision, on a worthy goal, it's a prime success strategy.

Chapter 17

Holistic Practitioner topics

22 overlapping names for the Habit Body

If you imagine there's still a great deal of confusion about our own Habit Body, you are correct. I estimate it will take 50-100 years from now for the Habit Body model to be taken more seriously and enter college texts.

Funny thing, even our confusion about ourselves, about our own psyche, is patterned. A famous poem exists about how we confuse ourselves and each other, "The Blind Men and the Elephant."

Consider a group of blind men. None of them have ever seen an elephant, nor any picture of an elephant. They are now in the same room as a live elephant, trying to understand it without any sight. With his two hands, each touches only one part of the elephant. At first each blindman believes his one small part of the elephant, the leg, the tail, the trunk, to be the true character of the entire elephant.

Guess what? College-educated males, in the period 1800-1950 got ahold of the rational, left-brain intelligence in our psyche. They proclaimed,

"Eureka! We found it! This one part is the whole of the Elephant of Consciousness!" Look no further! All other intelligences are illusory and must be dismissed!" This is how science became so one-sided, lop-sided and prone to endless creation of Frankenstein technologies.

Over-generalizing from one part, assuming the whole can be defined from only one part, is why humans at this time, are confused about their own Habit Body.

Full poem and its origins is here: (http://www.noogenesis.com/pineapple/blind_men_elephant.html) The poem also explains the "holy man's disease."

A sighted person looking more "spherically" at a healthy elephant, perceives multiple functions and aspects. Our etheric body is the origin of multi-tasking in human beings.

Because it encompasses multiple functions, 22 or more names exist for our Habit Body. See if you can add terms to this list:

- inner child, child within

- wounded inner child of the past

Habit Body 2nd ed ~ 210

- reactive emotional self

- "feelings and needs" in the NVC sense

- the 'Little Artist' of The Artist's Way

- animal self, animal nature

- The body's other half (from osteopathy)

- The organizing field (from osteopathy)

- growth body, the body electric, life force

- immune system of the body, 'immune system self'

- innate wisdom of the sum of your cells

- pre-conscious, subconscious, unconscious

- etheric body, etheric double

- gatekeeper of the etheric centers

- vitality, prana, chi

Habit Body 2nd ed ~ 211

- the body electric, life force

- pre-physical body

- archetype of the dense body Max Heindel

- Rudolf Steiner's "etheric double"

- memory body, Habit Body, habit hologram

- the one who sleepwalks

- morphogenetic fields (Sheldrake quoting Poppelbaum)

- neural default mode

- the "floating brain"

Q: Why are these "overlapping"?

A: Because our Habit Body is multi-tasking, just like our Immune System. It's difficult to separate closely related functions. Only left brain language, such as above, can create 22 names for the same thing.

22 FUNCTIONALLY equal names

All 22 terms for our child within are equal for several reasons. For one, they all point to the "bigger you," the 95% of your psyche outside the 5% where you spend much of your waking time.

Second, from Conscious Self's point of view, each one of these is connected with, contacted, communicated and negotiated with in exactly the same way, approximately:

acknowledgement > acceptance > curiosity > compassion >

forgiveness > negotiation

As in any nurturing parenting conversation with a three year old, identifying and negotiating new behavior is often the tail end of the conversation.

Thirdly, the mental age of all 22 named parts is approximately three years old. This is nothing to sneeze at. A three year old is plenty smart enuf to respond to what foodstuffs, supplements, sleep and lifestyle aspects are beneficial and which are detrimental.

4) Because our etheric body has at least a three year old intelligence, they all understand and can

distinguish between what is "TRUE for me now" and "NOT TRUE for me now." Yet, they won't voice a response unless and until you ASK.

5) Each and all 20 aspects can be communicated with in the same way. Self-muscle-testing, and now arm-length-testing, does nothing more, nor less, than expand on, and amplify, this inherent wisdom, so your inner three year old, and you, from the neck up, can communicate.

However you get a second opinion from your own internal source is a good way for you. The only way to go wrong, is not to try at all.

Conclusion ~ The above 22 names overlap to such a high degree, differences between them are insignificant except for technical and research purposes.

Q: How intelligent is my Habit Body?

A: "Intelligence" is an abstraction. What exists at the cellular level is simply "function."

Our cells don't know "intelligence." They understand "function."

The more functions a frequency level can perform the higher order it is. The more functions performed, the greater the "intelligence." The more complex the function performed, the greater the intelligence of the entity.

Our Habit Body is intelligent enuf to keep our food digesting, remember how to walk, remember how to speak local language; in fact, every repetitive learned behavior you prefer not to do consciously.

Please note this cannot all be chemistry, cannot all be neurochemistry; cannot all be genes. When we stick to "function" we remain closer to a body-based view of "intelligence" and are less likely to confuse ourselves. Full discussion and counter arguments in Balance on All Levels PACME+Soul.

Q: How can my lower helper self, my immune system, accomplish all its functions with the intelligence of only a three year old?

A: Any healthy three year old can respond to direct questions, phrased simply. It can respond "yes" or "no" to what it likes now. Its likes and dislikes can and will change over time. A three year old can respond to and know what is "TRUE for me now (beneficial);" or, "NOT TRUE for me now (neutral to detrimental)" within its natural function(s). Make sense?

Plants and animals have a much more narrow range of functions-intelligence. Their etheric body functions way more narrowly than the human e-body does. Human etheric body is much more variegated and diversified than the etheric bodies of plants and animals.

The intelligence of our etheric body, in its function as Immune System Self, is easiest to contact in our Small Intestine. Why? Because here, in the intestinal villi, 24/7, it is choosing which nutrients to assimilate directly into our bloodstream and which to let go by as not useful, unworkable or toxic. It is making choices of a very primitive nature but it is making millions of these choices every day. This is why the Small Intestine has been called "the brain at the other end of the body."

If our immune system did NOT have this level of intelligence in our small intestine, we would take into our bloodstream whatever was in our G.I. Tract indiscriminately.

Habit Body as "operating system"

Because our etheric body connects all these bodies into one whole, it is our natural "operating system" in the human experience.

In Windows 95 computer jargon, our Habit Body is the "shell program." It enables access to all functions and capabilities (apps), from the "front" of the system.

In 2005 computer jargon, our Habit Body is "firmware." Yes it can be changed, but it's more difficult than swapping software in and out; and, swapping firmware may or may not be advantageous. You better know what you are doing. Firmware is not a sandbox to experiment in.

Our Habit Body weaves together all the disparate functions of adult psyches together into one functional person who can both walk, chew gum and whistle Dixie all at the same time.

The Habit Body in Energy Medicine

Rudimentary single-muscle (arm-pull-down) muscle-testing in Applied Kinesiology (1965) then in Touch for Health (1973), began to open people's minds to the reality and intelligence of our sub- and unconscious in a way dowsing alone had not.

More people learned: a great deal of intelligence exists outside the comfortable campfire of the Conscious Waking Self--and--this additional intelligence cannot be accessed unless and until the individual ASKS--ideally within an ecumenical framework of 'God is my Partner.'

Muscle testing and later self testing opened the minds of Cultural Creative pioneers to natural intelligences inside each person, primarily invisible and "out of sight;" and how we can access them, understand them, upgrade and update them.

Outside of NLP, this was primarily not possible with talk therapy alone. Not until CEBT and Solution-Focussed Brief Therapy in the 1990s, did professional talk-therapist attention shift significantly to changing client behaviors per se, in client-centered ways (Skinner's 1930s Stimulous-Response Behaviorism was finally left behind).

Habit Body as etheric body

Our etheric body holds all our bodies together.

We need something to keep all our diverse human capacities together. The basic self has the job of keeping all our PACME conditioned capacities together "in mind" sub- and unconsciously.

This suggests the function of our etheric body as, "the web which has no weaver." The etheric keeps all your different bodies coordinated. Changes in any of your less physical, higher frequency bodies arrive down in the physical, over time, like raindrops ultimately regaining the sea.

To sum up: Consciousness is graduated from waking, thru dreaming to sleeping. The human psyche is graduated from waking, thru dreaming to sleeping.

What we call human nature, is no more nor less than a big collection of human habits.

Chapter 18

Behaviorism - taking habits seriously

1880-1955, scientists began studying psychology with the same methodical left brain tools Natural Science had applied to geology, anthropology, physics and so on. For the first time in left-brain-only-science, the difference between—who we are; and, what we do—was studied scientifically.

Early Behaviorists were very impressed with Pavlov's stimulus-response experiments with dogs. Could such results be replicated with other animals? With humans?

Redirecting behavior experimentally in animals and humans began to be widely studied in colleges. Skinner produced astonishing and successful results shaping the behavior of pigeons thru gradual approximations of a desired behavior.

Stimulus-response (S-R) theory says when something is done to us, we react. It says we only react; that's all we can do. It says we always react because something is done to us. If we feel cold, we move closer to the fire. If we are hungry we move towards food. If we are punished for stealing from the cookie jar we stop stealing. If we are driving and we see a red stop light, we stop.

Behaviorism theorized the whole of the human psyche can and must be reduced to cause and effect, stimulus and response. This hubris became a foundation of 19th and 20th century scientific-materialism.

S-R had a profound impact on factory production assembly lines. In the early decades of the 20th century S-R had a profound impact on centralized factory-style public K-12 education. The folly of this partial approach to life and learning is expressed in Chaplin's film, "Modern Times."

At their worst, early Behaviorists thought humans not much more intelligent than pigeons. They wondered, if we can shape pigeon habits easily, how far can we go with humans?

Some readers will know the 1920s-1930s were also the period of scientific hubris about eugenics, the worst errors of IQ tests, and selective breeding of animals and humans for dreamed-of optimal "supermen."

As you might expect, these experiments were Dr. Frankenstein-ish and today are little-studied. What was missing? Feeling was missing, healthy Feeling, all the intelligences of the right brain. Early hubristic Behaviorism was not client-centered, nor heartfelt, nor in the service of supporting clients' self-connection. Early Behaviorism has no interest in empowering clients to be anything more than good little cogs in a big machine run by elites.

After WW II, humanistic psychologists began conferencing in 1955. By the 1970s, a significant fraction of educated psychologists, psychiatrists and counselors were "peaking out," "dropping out" from the mechanical, deterministic models of the human psyche 1880-1930s. They became willing to explore Feeling with the same objectivity pigeon habits had been studied earlier.

Glasser's critique of Behaviorism

My favorite critique of Behaviorism is William Glasser's argument. Glasser says, yes, we respond to pain and pleasure. However the tail does not wag the dog.

Take driving a car and stopping at the red light. It's intellectually dishonest to say, "The light turns red, so we stop the car." The light does not come into the car and move the pedals to stop the car. It does not. The environment does not control us to this extent.

Rather we stop at the red light because we do not wish to get a ticket; we do not wish to have an accident; we wish to be safe; we wish to avoid the hassle of consequences for breaking rules. We choose to stop at the light. In driver training, if not earlier, we learned stopping at a red light on a busy street is by far our best choice. So we keep making the choice to stop--until it becomes a habit.

Consequently, despite the arguments of mid-20th century scientific Dr. Frankensteins, human behavior, more complex than Pavlov's dogs salivating at food, is caused from the inside, not from the outside.

Apart from accidents, in human affairs, the consequences of choice, of choosing, are usually far greater than consequences made on the level of stimulus-response.

We choose to change our behavior when another choice meets our needs better.

Q: So we should throw out early Behaviorism and all it stands for?

A: No, not quite. Let's give Skinner his due. Skinner, the hard-headed experimentalist, was in some ways a throw-forward to both NLP and self-muscle-testing.

Let's recall what Skinner was opposed to. In his time, Skinner was rebelling against the vague, patently subjective, sometimes absurd definitions of the psyche, common in the 17th, 18th and 19th centuries. Skinner did not support Freud's innovative psychotherapy. Skinner wanted something much more radical.

As a true left-brainer with no allegiance to Feeling, he considered "desire," "goals," "pleasure" and "values" to be mere abstractions. He criticized these words as "soft" and unscientific. Where was the repeatable experimental method for these words?

Skinner broke through the confused and confusing rhetoric of 18th and 19th century European philosophy, especially Romanticism. Skinner championed a much more direct (Extraverted thinking) approach to psychology. Skinner wished to limit psychology to only the realm of the sensory, the tangible, the objective and the measurable.

Skinner's approach was counterpoint to fuzzy Romanticism overwhelmingly influential in the century before him. Behaviorism was also a strong rebuke to the moralizing abstractions of the politically powerful European Catholic church in the two earlier centuries; when, all Church doctrine was based on Feeling, faith, belief, tradition.

In his day Skinner was the pendulum swinging back from familiar, comfortable fuzzy rhetoric about Feeling and language about "faith" which had no experimental method whatsoever. Subscribing to Romanticism and

NLP and self-muscle-testing had to break the same old bonds of faith-based psychology and faith-based Feeling as Skinner did.

Coming after Humanistic Psychology 1.0 as they did, in the 1970s, NLP and self-muscle-testing were also able to break the bonds of faith-based, Dr. Frankenstein, left-brain-only, scientific materialism, absent of healthy Feeling and healthy ethics.

Skinner challenged his audience not to accept all behavior as given. He challenged his audiences to consider what new habits could replace old dysfunctional habits. Skinner taught psychologists to think about behavior as malleable. More than Freud, Skinner encouraged psychologists to be more experimental and innovative. This was a crucial step towards NLP, self-muscle-testing and self-healing methods.

Self-testing as getting serious about habits

A long memory is needed to connect self-testing with BF Skinner. The similarity? Skinner desired to systematize behavior and break it down, chunk it down, into small enuf parts so human behaviors can be managed.

What intention do post-modern Solution Focussed Brief Therapists (SFBT), REBT therapists and Energy Medicine practitioners do? More or less the same thing.

In the 1970s, in some fields, resurgent Intuitive Feelers, using right-brain-only thinking, swung the pendulum too far to the right brain. The resulting excesses now look like caricatures and cartoons: Enuf empathy, enuf listening, enuf compassion can cure any ill, solve any problem. That's right brain. De-coupled from method and service to those less fortunate, compassion is empty.

In the 1980s, the pendulum swung back towards the middle, a balance of left~brain intelligences. CEBT-REBT, NLP, arm-pull-down testers and early SFBT therapists pushed back with a better synthesis of right and left brain counseling and therapy methods.

Sometimes this looks like: Slowing down, faced with a client's problem or physical pain, the post-modern therapist slows down. First be permeable and absorb the patron's input. What methods do I have to narrow down the complaint to make it as specific as possible?

The post-modern therapist also knows something the client is likely to be ignorant of: only part of the client wants to be healed. Usually the client wants to be excused from discomfort, usually from the neck-up.

The rest of the client, from the neck-down may be fearful of uncovering the actual primary causative factors. Why? Because if these are uncovered, a change in habits on one or more levels will be needed and asked for. Our Habit Body dislikes change. It wants only the predictable and the familiar. It wants to do tomorrow what it did yesterday. Almost always in physical healing, habits must change.

From the neck up we say, "I want to heal." From the neck down we say, "I have no skills and no desire to change my habits and comfort zones." Hence, many people are of two minds about their own problem, even if it may be life-threatening. If change does not feel safe and the likely outcome trustable, our Habit Body will resist even positive change.

When adequate and sufficient willingness to heal is present, uncovering specific, primary causative factors, is half the battle. The other half is testing solutions with the client. Individual solutions can also be tested directly with the patron's immune system and body, to see which remedies yield most bang for the buck (which are priority from the view of the body-immune system).

This intellectual rigor would have made Skinner happy. It can't be done with only right brain intelligences. We need the flexibility to go back and forth between right and left brain intelligences as needed. Whole-brainedness.

Even NLP's ideas of closely modeling new desired behaviors owes something to Skinner's focused observations of existing behaviors, to analyze behaviors down to their component habits.

That's why we say self-muscle-testing and Behaviorism are connected. Skinner's Behaviorism had the intelligence of left brain rigor. When combined with right brain intelligences, this produces the most effective results in counseling and therapy.

More discussion in Self-Muscle-Testing: Two Reasons to Use and 33 Beneficial Side-effects

Why are my muscle testing results unreliable?

Your muscle-level results may or may not be reliable. The bigger problem with beginners is almost always one or more of these:

- The question is vague and/or faulty,

- Your specific method of self-testing is archaic (Arm Length Testing is modern Best Practice),

- Your muscle level response is weak and tentative, easily misconstrued,

- The tester's sensitivity to inner changes needs practice.

The remedy for any of these is—practice.

The topic of testing difficulties is taken up seriously in Self-Healing 101! Awakening the Inner healer. In 3S Vol. One we discuss how self-testing results are repeatable but primarily within the domain of one person and the short time frame of here and now.

Muscle Testing as a Spiritual Exercise; [Build a] Bridge to Your Body's Wisdom may also be of interest.

Chapter 19

Birth and death,

our two greatest learning experiences

Birth is our greatest learning experience. We learn more in our first hour, after our first breath, than in any hour afterwards.

Our birth canal and first hour experience sets many habits in motion PACME. "As the twig is bent, so grows the tree."

Errors in perception about our Self, other people, the world, God can We have many perceptions, a few of them even accurate, valid and healthy, about what the human experience is and is not. We begin forming beliefs and expectations about life here, unconscious habits which can last a lifetime.

Joseph Chilton Pearce says in his *Magical Child* books and tapes, by age four, we have learned about 80% of what we are ever going to know about navigating thru 3D life. What additional wisdom acquired as adults, is mostly culture and semantics. These overlay whatever early memories, expectations and beliefs were laid down at birth and in our first four years.

In my Health Intuitive practice, sometimes I'm directed back to the first hour of life after the first breath. The individual's general attitude towards Self, Others, World, God begin here in the first hour. Impressions made--and not made--become part of memory.

Early impressions, decisions and perceptions are not always accurate. It's possible to uncover beliefs formed at this time and address them. You can re-choose what you believe is true for you here and what life can be like for you here in 3D.

In this regard, birthing babies in warm soothing water pools, ala Frederick Leboyer's, Birth Without Violence, creates a smoother transition from the starry realms into 3D materiality. This advantages babies by facilitating an unbroken transition of consciousness from the astral realms into the physical. This in turn creates opportunity to converge happy, graceful expectations about life here with their actual first few hours on Earth.

Death, the other great learning opportunity

Doctor and author Brugh Joy reports Edgar Cayce saying the fear and apprehension we feel leading up to physical death here parallels the fear we feel in spirit in the time leading up to our own physical birth into the Earth plane. We feel the same anxiety at both transitions.

Some clairvoyants report, after physical death, some people literally step out of their Habit Body, like an old snake skin. After death, the soul can recognize how many behaviors they were habituated to; which once away from the physical, now seem completely arbitrary, outworn and useless.

One friend of mine, after passing over, stepped out of many of their old ego and basic self habits, as if stepping out of a rigid cocoon. Once out of the body, she willingly let go of many old, outworn habits, a wonderful sight to behold. You don't have to wait until the day you die to release old habits no longer working for you. The passing over experience is simply one more opportunity to release things no longer workable for you.

Grief is our response when unconscious support is removed

"Even tho my (mother, father, sibling) didn't always get along or see eye to eye with me, deep inside the two of us loved each other and stayed connected." Personally, I have heard this several times from friends who have lost loved ones. This feeling of unconscious mutual support to and from blood relatives is widespread; tho, not universal in every case.

In a 1968 John-Roger Soul Awareness Tape released in 2017, J-R was speaking about grief when family and loved ones pass over. He voices a response people have when a loved one passes, "Who will I have who loves me?" Inside me I also heard, 'Who will I have who loves me, like they loved me?'

In any long-term relationship with mutual support, we acknowledge we are loved consciously. Lower in frequency, our Inner Child feels loved by them and loves them in return. Lowest in frequency, our unconscious feels loved by them and loves them in return. Grief is the breaking of habits of how we are used to getting our Love Tank filled.

When a loved one passes to the Other Side of Life, from the neck-up we know we won't be giving and receiving love with the person any more, on the Conscious level. We won't be connected with them as we were. There may be tears at this level--or not.

Sooner or later this realization sinks down to our Child Within. Our Inner Child grieves the loss of connection and giving~receiving with the loved one SUBconsciously. There may be tears at this level--or not.

If we don't hold back and complete our grieving, the realization of loss sinks down to our UNconscious. Our UNconscious grieves the loss of connection and giving~receiving with the loved one in our psyche's deepest levels. There may be tears at this level--or not.

How we give~receive loving and mutual support-- will now be different. We grieve a source of loving which was predictable, familiar, safe and trustworthy. We're on our own where we used to be supported.

Q: Does this ALWAYS happen when a family member passes over?

A: No. Some breaks in life between family members and loved ones can indeed be final and permanent.

Note how when final-permanent separations occur before physical death, many people grieve as if the other person had died.

How we respond to grief in stages is a very clear example of how our psyche is intelligent on multiple levels simultaneously, while adults are awake.

The good news? We can love and be loved on multiple levels simultaneously. I focus on the loving present today.

Physical death and your Habit Body

Physical death, after your last breath, is primarily releasing not our physical body but the lower frequencies of our Habit Body altogether.

If the inhabiting immortal-eternal soul has not prepared its mental-emotional body for this inevitability, at death, the ego feels like the totality of its sub- and unconscious support is being removed suddenly.

This is why people meditate, do yoga and other forms of self-connection and develop the higher frequencies of their Inner Game of Life.

The goal? This is up to you. I like the goal of continuing on until you can, with your eyes closed, imagine a rose, and feel it so real, you can smell it and hear birds chirping in the background.

Chapter 20

Frequently Asked Questions

Can self-esteem be instilled as a habit?

Establishing healthy habits of self-esteem is the primary task of infants, the very young child and prior to puberty.

To go further, we have to admit "self-esteem" is an abstraction for a basket of learned habits, beliefs and so on, PACME.

What is present body-based?

The strength--or weakness--of our self-esteem is primarily represented by our Conception Vessel in our Body of Meridians. Full Discussion in Meridian Metaphors manual.

Establishing competencies in as many fields, PACME, as possible and permitted and spiritually clear, is the primary task up to puberty. We learn and absorb healthy habits from worthy examples (parents, care givers).

Healthy-workable habits create a foundation of self-esteem. After puberty, healthy-workable habits of self-concept are the next goal. The sum, the combination of these two then can be drawn on as "self-confidence."

More discussion in two booklets:

You Have Five Puberties A Three Selves Journal on Children, and

Why Human Learning Style Reverses at Puberty; Self-esteem Plus Self-concept Equals Self-confidence

What about K-12 self-esteem education?

Between 1973 and about 1985, especially in California, self-esteem education came and passed thru mainstream culture as a wave. Not much was sustainable in K-12. Why? For many reasons, including

- Lazy teachers took advantage of it to do less not more lesson planning,

- Teachers were insufficiently trained

- Adult teacher-staff group process was largely ignored.

Can affirmations change habits?

Affirmations and positive thinking are useful. Why then are they of such limited use, for redirecting habits?

Could it be, we are not using them correctly? Could our beliefs and assumptions about habits and affirmations be faulty?

Let's talk about our Habit Body and self-healing.

Math and order of operations

Math is the easy way to see this more clearly.

Affirmations and positive thinking are clearly additive processes. As loyal consumers, we get stuck in only "addition mode."

The exact opposite math mode is required to make most progress in our Habit Body.

In math order of operations (PEMDAS) for the outer world, addition comes before subtraction. In the Inner Game of Life, subtraction comes first, then addition.

In our Habit Body, subtraction comes before addition. This is the order of operations, for virtually all adult self-healing, at this time.

Why? We need to take out the trash before we bring in the new goods. If we re-decorating the living room, what's the first practical thing we have to do? Get rid of the old rug, the old sofa, perhaps strip off the antique wallpaper. Then we can ADD, we can prime and paint the walls, then carefully select what new furniture (habits) we wish in our psychic environment. We probably want better lighting and more Light as well.

You want to turn the oceans back to fresh water? First you are going to need to get to that old Salt Mill, dysfunctionally grinding away on the bottom of the ocean, making useless salt, polluting all the connected oceans.

What's at the bottom of your psychic sea? To change unhealthy water back into sweet water, turn off the old Salt Grinders. This betters your chances to turn salt water back into drinkable water.

The muddy pond metaphor

If you had a pond with mud at the bottom, and you wanted to get the loose mud out, one way to get it out is by adding more clean water. More clean water pushes out the muddy water. When no more mud at the bottom—you're done.

Notice you're adding to subtract (reduce, eliminate) the muddy water.

This is how affirmations work.

But what if there is deeper mud this additive approach fails to address?

A more direct way to address a layer of mud is to scoop it out directly.

If your only tool is a spoon—then go by spoonfuls. If you have a snow shovel, then you can scoop out mud by the bucketful.

Most of our unresolved disturbances require subtraction first. Of all the four arithmetic processes, adding, subtracting, multiplying and dividing, subtraction is by far the most useful, effective and frequently used process in all self-healing.

Subtracting in the Habit Body

What Tools That Heal do you have in your Self-healing Toolbox? I hope you have Forgiveness; especially, self-forgiveness.

Readers can see a full protocol in *Forgive from Your Soul, Slow-Motion Forgiveness: the Missing Manual, Forgiveness 101 How-to Book* (New Directions In Brain Balance) (Volume 4)

How to become a happy ignoramus

Eventually, as we mature, we realize only a small fraction of our waking psyche is under our conscious, direct control. We realize 90% or more of our psyche is not-conscious. This is why wise persons often claim ignoramus status. They know there is more unknown territory inside them and around them, than territory known to them.

Funny misunderstanding about pets

The idea of a Habit Body in five dimensions PACME is necessary to understand one of the funniest things dog owners do. Have you ever seen a dog owner try to take a formal picture of their pet? They tell the pet to stay, the owner backs away to take the picture, and the pet follows them, or moves off or gets distracted. I have seen pet owners try to reset the dog in position for their photo shoot over and over; each time the dog will wander off more or less immediately.

What this tells us is many dog owners misunderstand how a dog can be intelligent; yet, less intelligent (lower frequency, less sophistication) than Conscious Self.

The technical answer? The erratic behavior of dogs asked to pose for their own picture proves dogs have no mental Habit Body. This is our capacity to form, remember and hold inside to an

Habit Body 2nd ed ~ 243

idea, a mental form. The intelligence of dogs is limited to encountering the outer sense world and primitive feelings.

Extra-credit pop quiz: Would pet fish owners be foolish to ask their pet fish to hold a pose for a camera? Why or why not? Compose an answer in your own words.

Some readers are going to be thinking now, "Wow, I over-estimate what my young child can do too."

Q: How can the difference between the intelligence of a child before puberty and an adult be characterized?

A: Easy. Classic, traditional fairy tales, not Disney, present to us the more limited dissociated way a child prior to the advent of Conscious Waking Self perceives the world and its actions. More research on this is called for re whether fairy tales align better with the child birth to age seven as opposed to birth to pre-puberty.

Without a clearer idea of how intelligences in us is "layered" (Multiple Intelligences 2.0) we are prone to assumptions and misunderstandings about intelligence below and above Conscious Self.

Another koan about pet owner behavior: Some people seem to love their pets more than they love their own child within. Why? They treat it better, feed it better food, love it more than they do their own inner child. Some pet owners will even tell you, "I'm nicer and more kind to my pet than I am to myself."

To answer this, think about kindergarten and how young kids learn new things.

Printed in Great Britain
by Amazon